Choose You This Day

Choose You This Day

The Gospel of Jesus Christ
and the Politics of Trumpism

PAUL C. McGLASSON

CASCADE *Books* • Eugene, Oregon

CHOOSE YOU THIS DAY
The Gospel of Jesus Christ and the Politics of Trumpism

Cascade Books
An Imprint of Wipf and Stock Publishers
199 W. 8th Ave., Suite 3
Eugene, OR 97401

www.wipfandstock.com

PAPERBACK ISBN: 978-1-5326-8573-6
HARDCOVER ISBN: 978-1-5326-8574-3
EBOOK ISBN: 978-1-5326-8575-0

Cataloguing-in-Publication data:

Names: McGlasson, Paul C., author.

Title: Choose you this day: the gospel of Jesus Christ and the Politics of Trumpism / Paul C. McGlasson.

Description: Eugene, OR: Cascade Books, 2019 | Includes bibliographical references.

Identifiers: ISBN 978-1-5326-8573-6 (paperback) | ISBN 978-1-5326-8574-3 (hardcover) | ISBN 978-1-5326-8575-0 (ebook)

Subjects: LCSH: Trump, Donald, 1946–. | Political culture—United States—21st century. | Christianity and politics—United States.

Classification: E911 .M40 2019 (paperback) | E911 (ebook)

Manufactured in the U.S.A.   07/17/19

"Choose you this day whom you will serve . . ."

—Joshua 24:15

"The ultimate measure of a man is not where he stands in moments of comfort and convenience but where he stands at times of challenge and controversy."

—Martin Luther King Jr.

Contents

Preface

The present work is written with at least three audiences in mind. It is written for Christians who are deeply troubled by the association of their treasured faith with the politics of Trumpism. It is likewise written for non-religious folk, who are concerned about the use—or misuse—of religion by Trump and his followers. And finally, it is written for supporters of Trump who may be having second thoughts on grounds of conscience.

I have not been shy in this book. I have tried to make a case fairly, objectively, and straightforwardly; but a case that is nonetheless seldom made, at least in the mainstream church. That it is seldom necessary to make is a good thing. But when it becomes necessary, it is imperative to remember that we are here critiquing a set of ideas, not a group of people. Nor am I here arguing against the religious right from the point of view of the religious left. That is simply to oppose one boundary language to another.

The Word of God's promise knows no boundaries; God's grace is everywhere.

I wish to express my deepest thanks to my good friend and colleague Mark Tranvik, who read this manuscript as it was being written and offered invaluable criticism and advice. Needless to say, any errors of fact and theological judgment remain my own.

Thanks also to Rodney Clapp, the editor, for fine work on our seventh book together.

Introduction

In the sixteenth century, Lutheran theologians made a theological distinction that would have a fateful history. Indeed, in many respects they simply made explicit a distinction that had already deeply impacted the church in an implicit way. Let me offer a brief explanation.

Martin Luther had insisted that salvation comes through grace alone, and is received by faith alone, which comes by hearing the promised Word of God. Despite enormous pressure, he would not retreat from that position; and the world now knows the result. The church divided. The Lutheran theologians were of course convinced that Luther had no choice. The issue he had seized upon was one in which the gospel itself was at stake. To retreat here was to lose everything. In such a situation, the church is in a state of confession (*in statu confessionis*). The notion of confession implies forgiveness of sins, and repentance is certainly part of a church struggle; but what they had in mind was different. The words of Jesus were in their ears and hearts: "Whoever therefore shall confess me before others, those will I confess also before my Father who is in heaven" (Matt 10:32). Standing by the truth in a time of desperate trial is not grounded in stubbornness, but in discipleship.

In fact, what distinguishes such confession from stubbornness is the other half of the theological distinction. There are some issues—plenty of issues, probably the vast majority of issues—upon which Christians can rightly disagree. You can fill in the blanks. Should we sing this kind of church music, or that kind? Should we send missionaries abroad or spend our efforts at home? Should we celebrate the sacrament by distributing the elements, or gathering around the table together as a congregation? And so on, and so on. Even profound theological issues can fall in this category. Does God suffer or not? Is eternity a kind of endless time, or is it qualitatively different, as God's own time? All of these issues—and countless others besides—they named "indifferent" (*adiaphora*). They did not mean unimportant; they simply meant, however important they may appear, and indeed truly are, disagreement over them should not divide Christians. That it sometimes does is a scandal, not a victory for the gospel. True wisdom lies in knowing when the church is in a state of confession, and when the church is facing issues that are "indifferent," negotiable.

Looking *backward* from the sixteenth century, it is clear that the distinction then made had already been operative, though never formulated precisely. In the early church, there was a wide variety of practice on a number of levels. Congregations in Antioch, Alexandria, Rome, Constantinople, and so forth, expressed a wide variety of Christian experience on a number of levels. There were different liturgies, nuances in biblical interpretation, different preaching styles, different church organizational structures, and so forth. These were all tolerated as *adiaphora* by the early church, though the word was not used. On the other hand, in a time of crisis, it was recognized that despite such diversity, there was a pattern of truth shared by everyone, a family resemblance in the affirmation of truth. And when that truth was tested, the church united and confessed, as it did for example at Nicaea, yielding the Nicene Creed, which is familiar today in the global ecumenical church. At Nicaea, the church found itself *in statu confessionis*, to use the later phrase, and it responded accordingly, with one voice.

Looking *forward* from the sixteenth century, the distinction would lie dormant, for the most part, until the church faced the most bloody and horrific century known to humankind: the twentieth century. We will describe the issues in detail in the chapters to follow; but what transpired was the temptation of one segment of the church—known as the German Christians—to follow Hitler and the Nazis, and to endorse their program on Christian grounds. There arose, in Germany, a group of Christians, called the Confessing Church, who invoked the theological distinction once again: we are *in statu confessionis*, in a state of confession. The gospel itself is at stake. Whether or not the church should support fascism is not the same kind of issue as whether we should sing traditional or modern music. It is not indifferent; it is essential. It strikes at the core. It is a call to discipleship. We will describe their response. And while we will not here examine yet another case, the same distinction was invoked in South Africa by the Dutch Reformed Mission Church against the supporters of apartheid, resulting in the Belhar Confession of 1982.

To summarize: while the distinction between truths that are negotiable, and truths that put the church in a state of confession, was made a technical one by Lutheran theology of the sixteenth century, it has in fact operated throughout church history. And there are three main periods of crisis (thus far) where it has shown itself vital: the early church, the time of the Reformation, and the struggles of the twentieth century.

The purpose of this book is straightforward. I here argue that the errors of American evangelical support for Trumpism have put the church, once again, in a state of confession, *in statu confessionis*. These are not errors that can be debated and discussed and then politely set aside. These are errors in which the gospel itself, and the gospel as a whole, is at stake. Indeed, we will endeavor to show that, at least in certain ways, the church struggles of the twentieth century, particularly in Germany, cast a long shadow into our own time. Donald Trump is not Hitler; that is not my point. Yet the theological rationale used by the German Christians to support Hitler and the Nazi agenda has, sadly enough, a family resemblance, a certain elective affinity, with American evangelical support for Trump. It is the theological rationale I am concerned to lay bare, and to which I offer a response.

Of course in the end the reader must decide for herself, or for himself, and so I have done my best to listen to the voices of the German Christians, and the American evangelicals, and not just describe them. As far as the German Christians are concerned, we have Mary M. Solberg to thank for making that possible. In her instant classic, *A Church Undone*, she translates the major texts of the German Christians into English for the first time. It is one thing to read studies of these issues; but hearing their views in their own voices adds, in my judgment, to the resonating echo one quickly detects with American evangelical support for Trump. That is not the purpose of her book, but it is an aftereffect.

We need to be clear who and what we mean by evangelical. In Germany, an evangelical (*evangelisch*) simply means a Protestant, one who follows the new gospel discovered by Luther. In England, an evangelical is one imbued with Wesleyan piety, a heart warmed by God, and is often synonymous with Methodist. Only in America does the word *evangelical* take on the reactionary political overtones it now has, and actually has had since its inception in the nineteenth century. So, when we speak in this book of evangelicalism, we are speaking of American evangelicalism. But we must be even more precise, more targeted. Since the change in immigration laws in 1965, whole new ethnic groups have entered the United States, and some have become evangelicals. These include for example some Asian Americans, and some Latin Americans. Yet neither of these two sub-groups of evangelicals support, in any way, the kinds of theology described in this book. They just don't, for a vast variety of reasons. Neither do African American evangelicals. So: when we are speaking of evangelicals here, we mean white American evangelicalism.

White American evangelicalism is espousing a set of views that can only be described as false doctrine. That is the argument I will make. In order to make it, I will listen to the voices of prominent representatives of the movement, people who represent the

Lord answered me and said: Write the vision; make it plain on tablets, so that a runner may read it . . . Look at the proud! Their spirit is not right in them, but the righteous shall live by their faith" (Hab 2:2–4). If this book calls for an end to Trumpism, it points to a new beginning far greater.

PART I

~~

The German Church Struggle

Historians will likely continue to seek well into the distant future fully to comprehend and explain the catastrophic inhumanity that was Adolf Hitler and the National Socialist Party in Germany. But one thing has long been certain. The reign of Hitler and the Nazis was the most barbaric, murderous event in human history. That it happened in the midst of the twentieth century makes the sheer brutality of hate all the more difficult to describe, much less to understand.

Why did Hitler set out on a course of such abominable inhumanity? His bitter and twisted views of the world were grounded in his boundless self-absorption. Hitler was a pathological narcissist. He was smarter than the generals; smarter than the professors; smarter than the scientists; smarter than the business elite. He alone was able to guide the destiny of the German nation, indeed the destiny of the whole world. Why? Because he had discovered the truth; that all life is struggle, all life is biology, all life is the anarchy of race.

For Hitler, the unending struggle of the races for supremacy was not the goal of history. History has no goal; history has no

1

meaning. There is only the struggle itself, which is self-grounded and self-justifying. If a race—the German race—wins the struggle, it only means that they were meant to win, nothing more. If another race, an inferior race, loses the struggle, they were meant to lose. There is no law outside the struggle. Certainly the international "law of nations" means nothing at all; it is merely to be deployed in the struggle, or set aside at will, depending on the circumstances.

And who decides the circumstances? Who determines when it is right to attack or retreat, to engage in diplomacy or to go to war in the service of national-racial supremacy? There is only one answer: Hitler himself. The struggle of the nation is his struggle, "My Struggle" (*Mein Kampf*). Hitler's is a world of blood and death, of weak and strong, of racial dominance. The only law is the law of power, and Hitler aimed to use that power to give the Germany people (*Volk*), the German nation, living-room (*Lebensraum*). Hitler knew that population numbers were growing. He also knew that German science was developing ways to feed the growing population. But he of course knew better than the scientists; he determined that the only way for Germans to live comfortably was to conquer and annihilate other peoples (mostly Slavs) and live on their now empty land. That he *could* do so (or so he thought) meant that he *should* do so; for the law of conquest was the only law of right. Science is politics; politics is science.

Only one thing held Hitler back, in the dark recesses of his own grotesque vision. There were elite institutions everywhere that would stand in his way: the state itself, universities, banks to fund his enterprise, the business community, and so forth. Life is biology; life is anarchy; so for Hitler, it was crystal clear in all its horror and shame that the one thing that held him back was the Jews. The Jews were the elite, the elite were the Jews. The Jews kept the world from seeing the law of struggle, the racial battle for supremacy which underneath the façade of "civilization" is the true secret of history. Civilization itself is of the Jews; so to persist in the struggle meant, in the end, to destroy both civilization and the Jews. Only then could the German race, the German *Volk*, take their rightful place as the true masters of the world, as led by Adolf Hitler. Such was the nightmare vision which determined the course of history during the dark years of mid-twentieth century history.

Among the institutions that were challenged to respond to the sheer bestiality of Hitler and the Nazis was the Christian church in Germany. Every institution was being coordinated into Nazi policies and designs by a process known as *Gleichshaltung*, the systematic repurposing of all life in Germany toward Nazi aims. The church was no different. The Nazis themselves were convinced that there would be no trouble from this quarter, that the church would surely go along. In the end, it is sad to relate, they were right. Nevertheless, the story is not without small victories, despite huge defeats, and these small victories need to be recognized and understood.

Thus, there were two broad responses: embrace the Nazis in the name of the gospel, or resist them. The first was the way of the so-called German Christians, the second the way of the Confessing Church.[1]

---

1. Just to be clear, we are limiting our attention in this study to two streams of theological writing and activism during the inter-war period (especially the 1930s), the Confessing Church and the German Christians. The *overall* church picture in Germany is more complicated, though it goes well beyond the bounds of this study to provide a full picture. There was, first of all, a large Roman Catholic presence in Germany, which made its own separate peace with the Nazis in the Concordat (*Reichskonkordat*) of 1933. It was controversial then, and it remains controversial now, but the issues surrounding it lay outside the special focus of this study. Similarly, though the Protestant church would eventually come fully to support Hitler en masse, during the period we are discussing church life was divided up roughly into three parts. Both the German Christians and the Confessing Church were a fairly small minority, of roughly equal strength. The larger majority of the church in Germany belonged to neither camp. Thus, there was a small contingent of active collaborators in the church; a small contingent of active church resisters; and in between stood the bulk of the church, waiting to decide. In the end, they would go along, if simply as bystanders. But that was later; the period we are describing was nothing short of a life-or-death struggle for the soul of the German church as it faced the peril of Hitler and the Nazi regime.

I

The German Christians

First some background. World War I left a profound impact upon the German people, but it was the Weimar Republic that most affected the church community, the protestant community in particular. Protestants in Germany were mostly middle class and rural folk. They lived comfortable lives, secure in stable truths, looking back on what they considered sacred moral values going back to the Reformation, especially to Martin Luther himself. Losing the war was bad enough; but the secular and republican nature of the Weimar Republic was the true threat to the church in Germany, as they perceived it. Gone were the verities of the past. Gone was their secure place in society, their social power, prestige, respectability, influence. Gone was the sacred story of their own history, to be replaced by nameless institutions of the present to which they felt little or no attachment. The liberal ideal of Weimar democracy left too much up in the air, too little secure in place for the church. In short, German Christians came out of the Weimar period utterly shaken to the foundations; and it is in this situation that the appeal of the German Christian movement came eventually to have enormous influence.

Who were the German Christians? They are not household names to most people today, certainly not in the United States.

Who has heard of Emanuel Hirsch, or Paul Althaus, or Gerhard Kittel? Yet these were three of the most well-known and established church scholars of their time, holding positions of the highest prestige, universally honored. There were able and dedicated pastors among the German Christians, who felt that the call of Hitler could not and must not go unheard in the very churches which they served. In short, the German Christians were a dedicated group of Christian leaders who believed that Hitler had been sent by God to lead the German nation forward according to the divine will. They saw it as their duty to follow Hitler; to teach others to follow Hitler; to tailor their message to the Nazi message; to organize the church itself as a Nazi church. If we are disturbed at this fact, of course we should be. But it is important to fully understand *why* they did what they did, and *how* they did it, in order truly to avoid making the same mistakes.

Their motives were rather straightforward: they yearned to be a part of this great new world order that Hitler was bringing about. The Nazi state was becoming a fact; they were eager to provide it with the theological justification it richly deserved. They knew in their hearts that Hitler was sent by God, and sought to inculcate in their congregations the absolute devotion and service warranted to him. They were convinced that the Christian message and Hitlerism were the same thing; and so they authored numerous tracts, articles, monographs, and statements, teaching this new version of the old faith, careful to point out that even Luther would approve. If asked, they would say that they were politically neutral; they would simply point out that they were German nationalists, clearly not even aware of the enormous self-contradiction. In short, they were complicit, and led others to the same horrific abandonment of genuine faith.

We should be clear: they were not terrorized by the Nazis into their complicity. Some of the Nazis expressed interest in Christianity; but Hitler showed little to no interest in the German Christian project, and certainly toyed with the church as yet another institution to be used and one day to be vanquished. The Nazis did not count on terror to push the church into compliance; they counted on *apathy*. They assumed that the violent chaos of their new regime would force individuals to retreat into the safety of their own finite worlds, disconnected to any larger reality. And so it happened.

Now, it is one thing to *describe* the German Christian movement, as necessary background. It is quite another to *listen* to their views, and to hear the voices in which they expounded them. It is to that we now turn.

Our first question is a simple but basic one. Upon what theological basis could otherwise decent Christian people—even distinguished pastors and scholars of the church—find themselves, not only in agreement with Hitler and the Nazis, but in active and enthusiastic support? Of course we ask the question with the benefit of hindsight; but we nevertheless must point out that the scurrilous and perverse evils of Nazism were scarcely concealed. So, upon what theological basis did a segment of the Christian community (the German Christians), and then finally the Christian community at large in Germany, come not only to accept but to embrace Hitler?

The answer is known as the *theology of orders*, and the architect was the distinguished Luther scholar and theologian Paul Althaus. According to Althaus, there is an *original revelation* from God separate from and prior to the Bible. Only in the context of that original revelation can the message of the Bible be truly interpreted and fully understood. There are certain facts of our common life together, known through common human experience, which form the basis of God's original revelation to humanity. Among those crucial facts are the realities of family, people (*Volk*), and race. Furthermore, the given moment of history in which we live is God's revelation of his will in the here and now. We can only believe in Jesus Christ from within this context: as members of a family, a Volk, a race, living in the historical moment that God has ordered. That is the theology of orders which virtually all German Christians shared.[1]

---

1. Althaus, *Die Christiliche Wahrheit*, 37–94.

What did that mean to Althaus himself? It meant seeing Hitler as a *miracle* of God, sent by God to save the German nation from the terrible trials of the Weimar Republic. It meant greeting his fellow church members: Heil Hitler! It meant seeing the entire program of Hitler and the National Socialists as the will of God for the German people at the present time, and offering his enthusiastic support. In his case, it did *not* mean joining the German Christians; as a highly trained professor of theology he found their formulations too imprecise. But his ideas were taken up enthusiastically into their literature and into their pulpits.

Here is how the "Original Guidelines for the German Christian Movement," written by Joachim Hossenfelder in 1932, makes use of the notion of God's "original revelation": "We recognize in race, ethnicity (*Volkstum*), and nation, orders of life given and entrusted to us by God who has commanded us to preserve them."[2] Notice, there is here no reference to the Bible or to Christ; rather, the orders of life are known from the experience of life, through which the living God grants full understanding of his will. And that will is *preservation*. Recall the shock to the rural and middle-class Protestant community flowing from the Weimar Republic, and the resulting fear of social and political dislocation; here is their answer. God does *not* want change; he wants us to preserve, to keep, to make what has been lost *secure* again. Exactly what that means we will discover shortly; but here is a taste: "For this reason race-mixing must be opposed."[3]

Again, the concept of orders of creation given in experience, prior to and outside of God's revealed will in the Bible through Jesus Christ, is used by Emanuel Hirsch, another distinguished academic theologian, and in his case an absolute supporter of the German Christian movement, Hitler, and the Nazis. Writing on the question, "What the German Christians Want for the Church," Hirsch states: "According to God's will, then, there are varieties of Christian thinking, speaking, and acting that are adapted to a

---

2. Cited in Solberg, *A Church Undone*, 49–50.

3. Ibid., 50.

8

particular people at a particular time in history."[4] God's will, here, refers not to his revealed will in Scripture, or in Christ, but to his original revelation through the orders of creation. And a taste of how Hirsch will use this concept further: "God has bound us together in natural community and order, as marriage partners, parents, and children, as coworkers, as comrades-in-arms, in the blood-bond of our nation, in the common destiny of our state."[5]

Before we seek to understand what form of Christianity was erected upon the basis of the theology of orders, one point should be noted, and it is a troubling one. It is more than likely that the *origin* of the theology of orders came into German theology from the *mission field*, or more precisely from German reflection upon missionary experience. Missionaries of all countries were learning in the early twentieth century that there are wide varieties of cultures and civilizations in the world. Mission scholars eventually concluded that it was crucial to translate the message of the gospel without importing Western cultural values not found in the Bible. German mission scholars in the 1920s and 1930s reached a very *different* conclusion. Every people, every culture, has their own special form of life, their own *ethnicity* (*Volkstum*). What these scholars brought back to Germany was just the *opposite* of what other mission scholars were teaching: Germans have the duty to *preserve* the spiritual essence of the *German* race in its own expression of Christianity, rather than the obligation not to *confuse* German-ness with the gospel. Hossenfelder, in the German Christian guidelines, puts it this way: "Based on its experience, the German Foreign Mission has long admonished the German people: 'Keep your race pure!'" and tells us that "faith in Christ does not destroy race, but rather deepens and sanctifies it."[6]

We come then to the second concept used by the German Christians in their theological support of Hitler and the Nazis, and that is their unbridled embrace of *nationalism*. Now, we think

---

4. Ibid., 113.

5. Ibid., 118.

6. Ibid., 50.

today of nations as areas of territory, bounded by lines as if on a map, within which are a variety of peoples and institutions. During this period in Germany under Hitler and the Nazis it was otherwise. The lines on a map mean nothing; in fact they can be contracted, expanded, or even erased forever at will. A nation is rather a people, a *Volk*, which is defined in racial/ethnic terms. It is essential to return to the non-metaphorical biological anarchy of Hitler: a nation is a race. A race is determined by the blood that flows through it. Every race shares a special line of blood. Insofar as it is a pure race, its blood is unmixed with "impure blood." Insofar as it is a true race, the blood is pure. The German nation are the German people, the German race, which shares the same blood with all true Germans, and which differs from the blood of all who are not German. The idea is of course in our time profoundly and grievously offensive; and so we struggle to understand how Christians could adopt it. But that is not what they did. They *embraced* and *celebrated* it.

Here is how Hossenfelder, in the German Christian guidelines, addresses the growing tide of German nationalism, as evoked of course by Adolf Hitler and the Nazis: "We want to bring to our church the reawakened German sense of life and to revitalize our church. In the fateful struggle for German freedom and our future, the leadership of the church has proven to be too weak . . . we want our church to be front and center in the battle that will decide the life or death of our people."[7] Front and center; for the German Christians, the role of the church is certainly not to *question* the new nationalism, or even to support it halfheartedly. The Christian church must be first in line in vigorously *promoting* and defending the rightful glory of German greatness. What, we might ask, about the universal church, the church that is everywhere among the nations of the earth? There *is* no such church: "We want a Protestant church with its roots in the people and we reject the spirit of a Christian cosmopolitanism. Through our faith in the ethno-national (*völkish*) mission God has commanded us

7. Ibid., 49.

to carry out, we want to overcome all destructive phenomena that emerge from this spirit, such as pacifism, internationalism . . . and so forth."[8] Perhaps we recoil at such a crude identification of the gospel with nationalist ideology. Or perhaps we hear something sadly familiar.

Hirsch presses the identity of Christian faith and German nationalism, if anything, even further. "How does the teaching on justification become a concrete way of life for a National Socialist Germany today? This is a question that we must answer if we want to guide today's National Socialist German into Protestant Christianity. He will never embrace faith in Christ if we cannot demonstrate . . . how Protestant and National Socialist morality and way of life merge."[9] Thus, for Hirsch, a version of Christianity, a political party, and a nationalist agenda are in essence identical. Hirsch has fully imbibed the poison of Hitler's biological anarchy. A nation is defined in terms of the purity of its blood: "Every human accomplishment and design is limited and bound by the natural character we bring with us into life. *If the blood is tainted, the spirit also dies*; for the spirit of both peoples and individuals arises from the blood" (Italics his).[10] Hirsch continues by bemoaning the dilution of German blood during the open democracy of the Weimar Republic, and concludes: "Our people's blood-bond was nearly undone. Had this process gone on fifty years more, the bearers of good, old, German blood would have become a minority among the leading sectors of our people."[11] It is the role of the church to join the Nazis in making sure that the *purity* of German blood is restored and maintained, and so insure the safety and greatness of the German nation. This is a *Christian* obligation. Notice again, the *fear* Hirsch expresses (with other German Christians) is that a majority is becoming a minority; and that the answer lies in resurrecting the glory of the past while going forward into a new future.

8. Ibid., 50–51.
9. Ibid., 108.
10. Ibid., 109.
11. Ibid.

Or again, we listen to the voice of a German Lutheran pastor, Julius Leutheuser, a leading spokesperson for the German Christians. In his document "The German Community of Christ," Leutheuser makes perhaps the most aggressive case—even more so than Hirsch, if that is possible—for the salvific role of the German people in the redemptive plan of God. His vision is without limits: "Responsibility for Germany and responsibility for the whole world are intertwined. Whoever does not love Germany, does not love the world either . . . Whoever is not prepared to die for Germany knows nothing of God's way of the cross in the world. Whoever does not believe in the resurrection of Germany, does not believe in the resurrection of God, despite the night and might of this world."[12] Thus, for Leutheuser, the German nation itself begins to take on the role of the saving life of Christ as narrated in the Gospels. He is adamant: "Loyalty to God and loyalty to Germany, faith in God and faith in Germany, love for our eternal home and love for our German home, love for our German brother and Christian love for our neighbor, striving for the kingdom (*Reich*) of God and striving for the German Reich, being a German and being a Christian—these notions are indissolubly linked with one another."[13] Leutheuser affirms the basic confession of the German Christian movement, which was spontaneously felt, he states, by all true Christians the day Adolf Hitler came to power in March of 1933: "One Reich, one community of faith, one people!"[14] Lest the lesson be lost, Siegfried Leffler (among many others) makes it quite clear: "In the person of the Führer we see the one God has sent, who sets Germany before the Lord of history. . . . [W]hoever wanted to live into the future had to align with him. One God, One People!"[15] Even in order to join the German Christians, one had to

12. Ibid., 325.
13. Ibid., 326.
14. Ibid., 329.
15. Ibid., 347.

be a member of the Nazi Party; and of course, on the application form, one had, in the sheer banality of Nazi evil, "to write legibly."[16]

To be German is to be Christian; to be Christian is to be German. To follow Christ is to serve the Führer; to serve the Führer is to follow Christ. To know the will of God is to do one's duty as a member of the German national race; to do one's duty as a member of the German national race is to do the will of God. These equivalencies—we would of course today argue that they are profoundly false equivalencies—were the common coin of Christian nationalism during this period.

The German Christians sought to coordinate all aspects of church life with Nazi ideology in order to insure that the new German church would rightly embrace the fullest expression of German Christianity. Hymns, sermons, church music in general, prayers, liturgies, all were reworked in such a way that the new order of German national greatness would be properly reflected. Nowhere is this more evident than in the stress—almost obsession, one might accurately observe—with the new cult of strength and power. If Christianity is to be true to the time, to the nation, and above all to the National Socialist movement, it must embrace *strength* and reject weakness. In the nature of the case, that meant for German Christians a new resurgence of *manliness* in all forms of Christian expression, and a suppression of anything redolent of the Weimar openness to women's emancipation and full expression. Women are to be wives and mothers at home; that is the new German Christian teaching. But there is more to it than that; there is a German Christian code of manliness that is a full-on embrace of Nazi views of what it means to be a person, or rather superhuman. The buzzwords scarcely concealed the underlying misogyny, and certainly openly expressed the deeply distorted Nazi view of what it means to be fully human. To live is to struggle and dominate; to be less than alive, less than human, is to be weak and succumb. That is the new German *Christian* version of the gospel.

---

16. Ibid., 177.

We listen, again, to Hossenfelder, setting forth the guidelines for the German Christian movement. According to the guidelines, German Christianity must reject the usual way of church politics in Germany, which "stands in the way of the noble goal of our becoming a churchly people. We want a vigorous people's church (*Volkskirche*), one that expresses the power of faith."[17] *Vigor, power, nobility*; these are the new catchwords of *manly* Christianity. Similarly, "We confess an affirmative faith in Christ, one suited to a truly German Lutheran spirit and heroic piety."[18] There can only be affirmation here, no calling into question German human potential. Here there is the heroism of the spirit that is the true greatness of faith. What Hossenfelder rejects is a squishy kind of love: "Mere compassion is charity, which leads to arrogance coupled with a guilty conscience that makes a people soft. We are conscious of Christian duty toward and love for the helpless; but we also demand that the people be protected from those who are inept and inferior."[19] The new, manly kind of Christian life has nothing to do with helping those who cannot help themselves. Real love is hard, not soft. Rather, if such people are truly helpless, they should be deemed inferior, and society should deal with them in a special way. Hossenfelder does not spell it out here, but it seems rather clear that he is expressing agreement with the Nazi view that "inferiors," the aged and chronically infirm, the mentally disabled, should simply be put to death, euthanized, which is exactly what Hitler did. That is "manly" love, according to the German Christians.

Arnold Dannenmann, in his "heroic" history of the German Christian movement, written in 1933, gives his own take on the new manly Christianity. Again, the text is laced with buzzwords that leave little room for interpretation. The new National Socialist Christian faith is one that is "truly great";[20] it has "immense

17. Ibid., 49.
18. Ibid.
19. Ibid., 50.
20. Ibid., 125.

significance";[21] it is a "powerful current"[22] flowing through the church and the people. To be truly Christian is to be a "brave fighter";[23] it is to "carry the battle forward";[24] it is to be a "fighter for the rights and duties of the German people."[25] To follow Christ is to "invest your blood";[26] it is to have "special sympathy for the German mother . . . and the responsibilities of the German woman."[27] The very definition of deep faith is to be an "uncompromising fighter."[28] Indeed, Dannenmann is quite proud of the fact that men in the S.A. and the S.S., the paramilitary arms of the Nazi Party responsible for countless acts of street violence, thuggery, and murder during the lead-up to the Nazi seizure of power, are *listening* to the pastors of the German Christians. The only reason they do so is because the pastors have true faith, which is to possess a lively, warrior spirit. Such pastors are "frontline fighters,"[29] "passionate warriors,"[30] "National Socialists at heart."[31] Everything must be done in the church in a "stormy fashion,"[32] for only so can the "strength of a vital movement"[33] contribute fully to the success of the German Reich and Adolf Hitler. Concludes Dannemann: "We know that the destiny of the German people is also the destiny of the German Protestant Church! But we also know that the destiny of the German Protestant Church is the destiny of the German people! They are woven into each other! Both must be vital

21. Ibid., 126.
22. Ibid., 127.
23. Ibid., 131.
24. Ibid.
25. Ibid., 134.
26. Ibid., 135.
27. Ibid., 136.
28. Ibid., 137.
29. Ibid., 140.
30. Ibid.
31. Ibid., 143.
32. Ibid., 150
33. Ibid., 162.

and strong!"[34] The manliness of the church is the manliness of the state; the manliness of the state is the manliness of the church. One can no more separate the one sphere from the other than one can separate the warp and woof of woven fabric. And they share the same character, which is the vital strength of true "manhood" as defined by Nazi ideology.

Not long after he wrote the guidelines for the German Christian movement, Hossenfelder wrote a pamphlet entitled *Our Struggle* (*Unser Kampf*), the title of course in conscious imitation of the earlier bomb-blast by Hitler, *Mein Kampf*. Here is Hossenfelder's version of the true life of a Christian people: "Whenever people live who are no longer willing to struggle, and then, ultimately, are no longer capable of fighting, life fades, and with it the good of the nation."[35] He is hardly subtle; to struggle means "gritting their teeth and balling their fists."[36] Hossenfelder, it should be pointed out, was one of the pastors praised for his relation to the S.A. and the S.S. He has an enemy in mind; it is the *elite* who have forgotten how to use their fists, and those are the "educated, in the German university."[37] Here in the university among the professors especially—he means of course Jewish professors—people have forgotten the manly Christian virtue of true *violence*. We can, says Hossenfelder, do nothing without Christ; it is precisely through him that "we will wrench our *Volk* up out of the abyss."[38] Indeed, the very definition of discipleship is this: "To fight on behalf of race and *Volkstum*."[39] He can only bemoan the fact that the church until now, until German Christian leadership has recognized its true calling through God's gift of Adolf Hitler, has been anything but manly: "The current church leadership is too soft and not aggressive enough . . . We want a combative church, courageous in faith,

34. Ibid., 162.
35. Ibid., 233.
36. Ibid., 234.
37. Ibid., 235.
38. Ibid., 242.
39. Ibid., 248.

that brings strength and comfort, joy and freedom to the German people of this new era."[40]

A final voice needs to be heard in our consideration of the "manliness" of the German Christian gospel, and that is the voice of Ludwig Müller, who had been appointed as the leader of the Nazi church, the National Bishop, or Reich Bishop. Indeed, more than *his* voice needs to be heard. To support the "manliness" of *Müller* himself, his supporters circulated stories that he was a "ladies man," that he was somehow sexually unconstrained by the artificial limits of bourgeois marriage. The Reich Bishop! But such was the bizarre and troubling doublespeak of the time: piety must be manly, manly men must be capable of having more than one woman, therefore pious Reich Bishop Müller must be something of a "player." But far more famous, or notorious, was his contribution to the German Christian versions of the Bible. Müller presented what he considered a truly "Germanized" version of the Sermon on the Mount, from which we can here only provide a few sample selections. I will provide the New Testament words for comparison.

Jesus said, "Blessed are those who mourn, for they will be comforted." Müller provides the Germanized version: "Happy the man who bears suffering like a man. He will find the strength never to sink into despair."[41] Be a Man, and you will overcome! Jesus said: "Blessed are the meek, for they shall inherit the earth." Needless to say, in the new era when meekness is despised, this will require true Germanization: "Happy the man who is always sociable. He will amount to something in the world."[42] Be a Man, and you will succeed! "Blessed are the peacemakers," becomes, in true *völkisch* fashion: "Happy are those who are at peace with their fellow Germans; they do God's will."[43] Be a Man, and get along with your kind! Those who are "persecuted for the sake of righteousness"

40. Ibid., 248.
41. Ibid., 386.
42. Ibid.
43. Ibid., 387.

suddenly take on a very different aspect: "Happy are those who live and work honestly and faithfully, and yet are persecuted and slandered—they will have communion with God."[44] Be a Man, and God will stand by you! The command of Christ to "turn the other cheek also" to one's enemy is offered anew to the German church and people: "If your comrade, in his anger, should hit you in the face, it is not always right to hit him back. It is more manly to preserve a superior calm. Then your comrade will probably be ashamed of himself."[45] Be a Man, and keep your composure! In every instance, whether subtle or overt, the radical call of discipleship is turned into a kind of ethical pabulum fit for a bad speech given to a meeting of the Elks Club (with apologies to the Elks).

Such versions of the new, manly Christianity of the German Christians could be multiplied endlessly. The language, and the ethos, is written into the Nazi creed, and therefore into the German Christian creed, regardless of it antithesis to the Christian confession. One point I think should be added. There is certainly a clear hatred of women, not concealed, but rather openly manifest in the various German Christian manifestos. The degradation of women is a pronounced element of the cult of manliness, and deserves utter condemnation. But so also is the degradation of genuine masculinity. There is nothing truly masculine in such "manliness"; in the end, the *human* simply disappears altogether, along with the Christ who defines it.

We turn now to the deeply troubling embrace by the German Christians of a virulent *racism*, expressed primarily in abject and hateful anti-Semitism. Recall that Hitler saw Jews and Judaism as the single primary enemy standing in the way of his conception of biological anarchy. Only Hitler knew the secret of history: life is a blood war of the races for supremacy. To know this truth is to live this truth. *Civilization* however conceals this truth from the unwary, and therefore stands in the way of truth. And civilization is of the *Jews*. Therefore, to engage in the life or death struggle of the

44. Ibid.
45. Ibid., 389.

salvation of the German race, it is without doubt necessary—so Hitler thought and pronounced on every occasion—to *annihilate* the Jews, all of them, as a people. Anti-Semitism of course was hardly new in European history, least of all within the walls of the church; but the intention, indeed eventually the plan, to destroy Judaism entirely, necessitated the invention of a new word: *genocide.* Perhaps most well-meaning people today, certainly most Christians, would expect the church in Germany at the very least to *protest*, if not actively to act *against* the Nazi plan. They did not. They joined the chorus—with but few exceptions—with full-throated enthusiasm, as inconceivable as that may seem.

Again, it is helpful and important to listen to the voices of German Christians as they defend anti-Semitism as the official *Christian* position. We will start once again with Hossenfelder, and the basic guidelines for the German Christian movement. There is a grave hazard in sharing the gospel of Jesus Christ with Jews: "In the mission to the Jews we see great danger to our people."[46] What is the danger? Is it the recognition that the Jews are still the covenant people of God, side by side with the church? Hardly. The issue is racism, brutal and hateful: "It is the point at which foreign blood enters the body of our people. There is no justification for its existing alongside the foreign mission. We reject the mission to the Jews as long as Jews have citizenship, which brings the danger of race-blurring and race-bastardizing."[47] Hossenfelder is fearful of a mission to the Jews because they might respond! And if they did, in his biological/racist conception, foreign "blood" would enter the "pure blood" of the church. What if a Christian falls in love with a Jewish person, and vice-versa? "It is especially important to prohibit marriages between Germans and Jews."[48] Again, we need to remind ourselves, this is being offering as *church teaching*, not Nazi propaganda, though obviously it becomes difficult to

46. Ibid., 50.
47. Ibid.
48. Ibid.

distinguish the two. The separation of the "races" is a Christian duty; that is the teaching of the German Christians.

Emanuel Hirsch, if it possible, is even more hateful, and certainly more focused, in his attacks on the Jews—from a German Christian point of view. Indeed, for Hirsch, the Old Testament belongs to the Jews, and therefore the Christian church must forever sever itself from the Old Testament. Hirsch argues that the only reason that the church keeps the Old Testament at all is because Jesus himself obviously holds the Old Testament in high regard. But that is not enough. Paul teaches us that the gospel is the end of the Law; and that means that the Old Testament is now forever useless to the Christian church, a Jewish book to be handed over to the Jews as foreign to the church as the Jewish people themselves. Indeed, Hirsch goes so far as to say that elements of "Old Testament-Jewish teaching" are "devilish";[49] and they are certainly utterly untrue. It is simply forbidden for the church of Jesus Christ to take the Old Testament as "a Holy book."[50]

By far the harshest defense of anti-Semitism coming from within the German Christian movement was offered up by Gerhard Kittel, a well-known biblical scholar to this day, editor of the internationally renowned *Theological Dictionary of the New Testament,* which is certainly found in every major seminary and university library, and doubtless also on the shelves of many working pastors and scholars worldwide. Kittel is not *reacting* to the issue of anti-Semitism; he is clearly *driving* the conversation forward, promoting a Christian anti-Jewish program fully within the orbit of Nazi policy. All on the basis—so he is quite clear—of the Christian gospel. He writes a pamphlet in 1933 that quickly goes through three editions, and he spends much of the Nazi period doing absurd research on pseudo-racial theories. In short, the detour into the National Socialist camp destroys the integrity of Kittel's lifework as a New Testament scholar, which is never rehabilitated. He died shortly after World War II, in 1948.

---

49. Hirsch, *Jesus und das Alte Testament*, in *Gesamalte Werke 32*, 166.

50. Ibid., 167.

The pamphlet is entitled "The Jewish Question" (*Die Juden-frage*). Even the title is an anti-Semitic trope; why after all should there be such a thing as a "Jewish question" at all? Why not a German question, or an English question, or a Scandinavian question? Simply to announce the "question" is already to define a force-field of hate. According to Kittel, the question is a very unsettling one for most German people: "Among the questions currently arising from today's German political situation, the Jewish question is the one that engenders an intense sense of insecurity and helplessness among many serious-minded people . . ."[51] He means insecurity among *Germans*, not among Jews. The sense of helplessness stems from a simple fact that cannot be ignored or denied: "there has been something about the situation of the Jews and their influence in Germany that has not been quite right."[52] Once again, this is an anti-Semitic trope; no details are ever given in such instances, only the vague generalities of prejudice and defamation. But no matter, Kittel plows on with his "scholarly" treatise. Kittel is concerned that some people simply don't have the right perspective on how deeply important the "Jewish Question" truly is. They have doubts; they have quibbles; they wrestle with details. And so he offers in this pamphlet what he considers the *definitive* answer for the German nation. The only way to convince *everyone* in Germany that the Jews are indeed a real problem to be "solved" is to put the whole question in *Christian* terms: "The true and complete answer can only be found if the Jewish question is successfully supported in religious terms and the fight against Judaism is given a Christian frame of reference."[53] The Nazi fight against the Jews is right, but it needs to be made a *Christian* fight if it is to be fully convincing, and that is what Kittel aims to do.

A critical German scholar, Kittel typically takes up the issue in a series of steps for consideration. First of all, it cannot be solved if it is simply referred to *individual* Jews; whatever solution

51. Cited in Solberg, *A Church Undone*, 204.

52. Ibid.

53. Ibid., 205.

is reached must apply to the Jewish people *as a whole*: "If I want to resolve it, or if I want to evaluate a proposed resolution to it, I may not look first at individual Jews. It is not about whether individual Jews are or are not upstanding Jews . . . The Jewish question is absolutely not a question of individual Jews, but rather a question of all Jews, of the Jewish people as a whole."[54] Keep in mind that this is written in 1933, a veritable template of abominable horrors to come. He is not seeing Jews as individuals, but as a race, and therefore no longer as human persons. Kittel sees only four possible solutions (from a "Christian" perspective).

The first, stated matter of factly by Kittel, is the total *extermination* of all Jews. That, he suggests, would solve the problem, simply by eliminating the Jewish people from the earth. So why not just do it? The only problem he raises is that it is impractical. Many pogroms have been tried, in Russia for example, but none have ever fully succeeded. Extermination is wrong because it is in actual historical circumstances it will not work: "Killing all Jews is not mastering the task at hand."[55] Needless to say, on this issue, Nazi policy will eventually come to disagree.

The second option is to deport all Jews in the world to Palestine. If all Jews are, as it were, *quarantined* in a single location, then the Jewish question is solved. Once again, the objections raised by Kittel are practical in nature. First, there are plenty of Jews who have no interest in migrating to Palestine. Second, it would be unfair to the people already living in Palestine, who would be unfairly treated by the Jews; it is remarkable, I might add, that Kittel shows no sense of irony in stating his concern for Palestinian inhabitants, while blandly discussing the wholesale destruction of the Jews. And finally, there is just not enough room in Palestine for all Jews to live there. The solution will only work if the *entire people* are involved; leftover communities of Jews in Europe and elsewhere make this solution worthless.

54. Ibid., 206.
55. Ibid., 207.

The third possibility is to allow the Jews to assimilate; that is, freely to circulate among the German people, and simply to become true Germans. There is a severe impediment to this solution, which renders it utterly impossible. Inevitably, there will arise marriages between Jew and non-Jew, so-called "mixed marriages." The result is a catastrophe: "Countless mixed-bloods (*Mischlinge*) pervaded the body of the German people. Because in many cases they bore strongly Jewish features, they strengthened the influence of the Jewish element on the body of the people."[56] For Kittel, the reason assimilation won't work is that the result is not to make Jews more German, but to make Germans more Jewish, which is the one thing above all to be avoided. The pagan Nazi policy of biological racism is here quite evident, though it is being offered as sure Christian teaching.

The final possibility—which Kittel for the moment at least recommends—is to allow Jews to stay in Europe, but as a people apart, both figuratively and literally. That is, they must live in a ghetto. They are to be treated as *guests* in Germany, not citizens, and allowed free movement only within the confines of the delimited Jewish space. Kittel feels free to define Judaism itself for Jews: "Real Judaism remains true to its symbolic being as a restless and homeless sojourner wandering the earth."[57] It clearly does not occur to him to ask whether Jews themselves agree with *his* definition of their very existence.

We are of course rightly appalled—the word is not strong enough—by these voices of support for virulent anti-Semitism coming from within the Christian community, the same anti-Semitism that fueled so much of the bonfire of Nazi ideology and atrocity. It should be frankly acknowledged that the German Christians were hardly the first within the Christian community to express and act upon anti-Semitic views. Anti-Jewish polemic is found in the earliest levels of Christian theology in the church, based upon the doctrine of supercessionism, which teaches that the church

56. Ibid., 213.
57. Ibid., 219.

simply *replaced* Israel in the divine economy of grace. Such a position in fact directly contradicts the argument so carefully laid out by the apostle Paul in Romans 9–11, but that argument would not be fully heard again in all its richness until after the war. Similarly, the Nazis used some of the late anti-Jewish writings of Luther to bolster their murderous program, though it is clear that Luther, while hardly defensible, nevertheless careful warned against harming Jews physically in any way, and was obviously (and sadly) here simply unable to overcome the prejudices of his own time, shared even with a humanist like Erasmus. And of course the outbreak of a new "atheistic" communism—"bolshevism"—was everywhere ascribed by the Nazis and the German Christians to "the Jews," though it had wide appeal to a newly industrialized Germany. The street battles between Nazi brownshirts and communists were, in the twisted Nazi psyche, a war against Jews. Indeed, Christian anti-Semitism in Germany was so widespread that it was in some sense not a moral choice, not a moral decision, so much as a moral *capitulation* to the prevailing climate of hate and bigotry. It takes a decision, a choice, *not* to hate; the hate comes all too easily. Anti-Semitism in Germany was a *traditional moral value*, and Hitler proudly embraced and endorsed it.

We ask, finally, about the figure of *Jesus Christ* within the framework of German Christian teaching. He is not often referenced in the various pamphlets, studies, confessions, and statements of the movement. It is for more common to hear references to Luther, though clearly a Luther that has nothing to do with the historical figure Martin Luther, but a Luther assimilated to Hitler's vision of a German Reich. Indeed, it is far more common to hear references to the "miracle" of Hitler himself, who is imbued with a profound faith in God, a notable piety, who carries a Bible and prays daily, and so forth, than it is to hear of Jesus of Nazareth, the Savior of the world. When it comes to who knows and rules the destiny of Germany, the answer is always the same: Hitler. It is never Christ. This is how Hitler is spoken of by the German Christians: "In the person of the Führer we see the one God has sent, who sets Germany before the Lord of history, who calls us from the worship of words, from the cult of the Pharisees and the Levites . . . This is why we who are and wanted to be pastors chose him. His struggle, his triumph, were just as decisive for the church as for all other areas of German life."[58] These are of course words of praise and worship, taken, often verbatim, from liturgical praises of Christ; but they are now transferred to Adolf Hitler, savior of the nation and the church. And Luther is referred to, not on the basis of his theology or witness to Christ, but as the *forerunner* of Hitler, who paved the way for the Germanizing of Christianity by translating—Germanizing, rather—the Bible. The Bible became a "people's book in the true sense of the word at a particular time, certainly at a unique moment of spiritual development. This was the work of Martin Luther."[59] Luther was the founding father; Hitler is the living Savior of Germany. It goes without saying—perhaps it needs to be said clearly—that this portrait of Luther is rubbish.

So what of Christ? There is of course a distinct problem for the German Christians, which will have occurred to many readers by now. Jesus of Nazareth was Jewish. How can this Jewish carpenter's son from Nazareth be of any use to the German Christian movement? In one of the most remarkable pieces of sleight of hand, the German Christians attempted to solve this problem with a "historical hypothesis" that was neither historical nor a true hypothesis. It was rather a piece of propaganda needed to keep the figure of Christ relevant, at all, to German Christianity. They argued, quite simply, that Jesus was *not a Jew*. The German Christians called their historical theory "the Galilean hypothesis," though it was not hypothesized by a historian, but by the architect of Nazi racial thought, Houston Stewart Chamberlain. Almost unaccountably, it was given credibility by being sponsored by Walter Bauer, like Kittel a highly regarded biblical scholar, whose New Testament Greek lexicon is, again, on virtually every shelf of those who read the New Testament in Greek. Galilee, so the argument ran, was actually not a Jewish province at all, but was Gentile. Being born in

58. Ibid., 346.
59. Ibid., 282.

Nazareth of Galilee therefore guaranteed that Jesus was not Jewish. He can be relevant to the new German Christianity for one simple reason: "he had not a drop of real Jewish blood in his veins."[60]

It goes without saying that such a view has no scholarly support today; indeed, even at the time it was a bizarre and twisted narrative, despite support from Bauer. The lesson is not that the view did have some scholarly support; the lesson is rather that even notable scholars were pulled into the swirling vortex of German Christian racism, despite their otherwise sterling credentials. Racism does not spare the learned. In the end, it spares no one. Only grace conquers all hate.

One final issue needs to be addressed in our consideration of the racist policies of the Third Reich. It is a deeply troubling consideration—or should be—to those of us who live in the United States, and honor its national heritage. But it is necessary to address the issue, for, as we shall see, we are otherwise operating in a kind of historical echo chamber without realizing it. Let me explain.

When the Nazi lawyers gathered in 1934 to 1935 to frame the infamous Nuremburg Laws—two laws which forbade citizenship to Jews and forbade sexual intercourse between Jews and Germans— they cast about for models in constructing the laws. Most of the German textbooks on international legal rules for citizenship were devoted to describing who *could* be a citizen; but the Nazi lawyers were interested in defining who could *not* be a citizen. Where to turn for help? The fact is, they turned to various elements in the federal and state legal codes of the United States. In particular, various racist laws concerning blacks in America provided a model—not an exact formulation, but certainly an inspiration—for how these Nazi lawyers went about constructing the laws defining Jews *out* of German society. There were four major sources. Already Hitler had shown great interest in the treatment of the Native American population during American history. Here, he argued, was a white people who simply drove a non-white, native people off the land

60. Ibid., 441.

in order to gain *Lebensraum* for themselves, whether by broken treaties, or simple forced and violent expulsion. Second, there was great interest shown by the Nazi lawyers in the 1924 Immigration Act. Without any doubt it was clearly designed to allow into the United States Northern Europeans, and to keep out Southern and Eastern Europeans, and certainly Asians. In short, while it accomplished the legal goal of restricting immigration, it did so in a way that was blatantly racist along the lines of white supremacy. Third, there was the well-known Jim Crow system, which rested on the perpetual threat of lynching to remain in force. And finally, the Nazi lawyers were able to find countless examples of laws on the books preventing "miscegenation" between whites and blacks. Such laws routinely defined what it meant to be "Negro," such as this Maryland statute: "All marriages between a white person and a Negro, or between a white person and a person of Negro descent, to the third generation . . . are forever prohibited, and shall be void; and any person violating the provisions of this Section shall be deemed guilty of an infamous crime and be punished by imprisonment in the penitentiary."[61] The Maryland law could be multiplied endlessly, and the Nazi lawyers had the texts in front of them as they constructed their own infamous Aryan laws. One crucial point needs to be stressed, lest it be missed: American immigration law was a fruitful source of inquiry for Nazi racial policy. Immigration law is a mirror of the fairness of a society, or indeed the lack of it.

Now, several point need to be stressed. First, American policy was *not* equivalent to Nazi policy, even in the 1930s, before the onset of the Holocaust. The Nazis constructed a murderous authoritarian state to enforce its racial regime; the United States relied on lynching to enforce a system of Jim Crow. There would be terrifying and despicable murders of innocent African Americans in the United States; there would be vile racial degradation; there would be the oppression of an entire race due to the constant threat of death by lynching; but there would be no Holocaust, no murder

61. Whitman, *Hitler's American Model*, 79.

of an entire population. That does not make American racism less immoral than German Nazi racism; it simply makes it different in form. Still, second, it needs to be stressed again; when the Nazis looked for legal "help" in constructing the legal framework for persecution (and eventual annihilation) of Jews in Germany, the *only legal system* that gave them help in "defining" a race, excluding a race, and dominating a race, was the American system of racial injustice.

And now a third point, which is perhaps the one most relevant to this brief study. There are clear echoes between German Christian support for Hitler and conservative evangelical support for Trump. Of course Hitler is not Trump, Trump is not Hitler. Such a facile identification is too simplistic, too easily dismissed, and trivializes both history and the problems at hand today. But then how to account for the similarities that remain, and that will be considered more fully in our next section? Obviously the Nazis are not copying Trump; history runs forward not backward. And it is too facile to argue that Trumpism is a copy of Hitler, though of course the Nazi fringe element is always there, even now. But there is a third option, which is to my mind fully convincing. And that is this: both Nazism then, and Trumpism now, were and are drawing on the same American traditions of racism that, despite the best efforts of the civil rights movement, remain sadly intact. The racist immigration laws of the past; the racist components of social engineering; the racist violence that was always just below the surface, even when it did not break out into the open, which it often did; these are elements of American history that at the very least inspired the Nazis, and at the very least are scarcely hidden in the conservative evangelical support for Trumpism.

And it is time to say: enough is enough.

2

The Confessing Church

The Confessing Church arose in direct reaction to, and confrontation with, the German Christian movement. While it was active on a wide variety of fronts, the most important work of the Confessing Church was the confession known as the Barmen Declaration of 1934. We will give most of our attention in this chapter to the contents of the Barmen Declaration; nevertheless, some background information is once again helpful.

If the immediate cataclysm standing behind the German Christians was perceived to be the Weimar Republic, without doubt the great catastrophe for the Confessing Church was World War I, and more particularly widespread Christian support for the war. During the early decades of the twentieth century, Europe was still conceived to be the center of a realm of "Christendom," with the Islamic Ottoman Empire to the East, and the (ultimately) self-described atheist Soviet Union on the periphery. And yet, this great realm of Christendom imploded in utter self-destruction, during one of the most hideous orgies of mutual human degradation in history. Trench warfare in France produced nothing but death and misery. On one side, Germans were praying to the Christian God for a German victory; on the other side, the English and French were praying to the *same* Christian God for victory against the Germans, and so forth. Sadly, many would come to see the blatant and facile hypocrisy of the Christian church in Europe, and leave Christianity altogether. But a few would dig even deeper to the theological roots of that hypocrisy, and that effort would eventually lead to the Confessing Church, indeed to an entirely new *epoch* in theology. The drive for a new approach in the whole of theology was led by the most important theologian of the age, Karl Barth.

A theological student in Germany just prior to the war, Barth was absolutely shattered by the easy and enthusiastic Christian support for the war, not least by his own theological teachers: "a whole world of exegesis, ethics, dogmatics, and preaching, was shaken to the foundations, and with it, all the other writings of the German theologians."[1] For Barth, Christian support for the war in Germany was a symptom of deep-lying theological assumptions that had to be exposed, critiqued, and eventually replaced by nothing less than an entirely *new* approach to the task of theology and preaching. His concerns took him directly to the Bible, and would eventually produce the epoch-making *Commentary on Romans*, published just after the war. But already during the war, Barth was struggling toward a fundamentally new approach. In 1916—in the middle of the war, that is—he gave, for example, an astounding lecture entitled "The Righteousness of God." The righteous God is on the side of the Germans, some are saying; the righteous God is on the side of the English others are saying; but what, one must now ask, does the Bible say? Everyone seems quite assured that *God's* righteousness, and *our* righteousness, are the same thing, or run along the same axis of moral alignment, and so they are assured. Barth responds: "No, it is not true! There is above this warped and weakened will of yours and mine, above this absurd and senseless will of the world, another which is straight and pure, and which, when it once prevails, must have other, wholly other, issues than we see today."[2] This will, which is the will of *God*, cannot in any

---

1. Busch, *Barth*, 81.
2. Barth, *Word of God*, 13.

way be correlated with the desires and designs of human intrigue, national or personal. Only the will of God is truly righteous, and he wills nothing less than *a new world*. Barth is convinced that it is this basic theological error—of confusing human projects with the living will of God—that is driving Europe into utter ruin: "We stand here before the really tragic, the great, fundamental error of humankind. We long for the righteousness of God, and yet we do not let it enter our lives and our world—cannot let it enter because the entrance has long since been obstructed."[3] That "obstruction" is the terrifying error—the "Christian" error in European theology of the nineteenth century and before—that God and human projects are to be understood in a common framework, as if God is to be captured in a human web: "And we are Christians! Our nation is a Christian nation! A wonderful illusion, but an illusion, a self-deception!"[4] For Barth—and many who would join in a quest for a new Christian theology during and after the war—the new key was to *let God be God*: "He is right and not we! His righteousness is an eternal righteousness!"[5]

Between the first World War and the advent of Hitler and the Nazis, this new approach to theology—it would later be dubbed "neo-orthodoxy," though Barth never used the word—was slowly hammered out in a series of monographs, books, commentaries, and essays, not only by Barth, but by others who shared his concerns. Our aim here is not to chart the course of this new theology, but to set the background for the Confessing Church. Consequently, only one of those comrades of Barth needs to be mentioned here, and given further attention below, and that is Dietrich Bonhoeffer. Bonhoeffer was a generation younger than Barth; Bonhoeffer was Lutheran, Barth was Reformed. Nevertheless, the two came to share bonds of friendship and theological concern that would be absolutely crucial in the formation of the Confessing Church. Both despised the rise of Hitler; both grew

3. Ibid., 15.
4. Ibid., 20.
5. Ibid., 23.

increasingly distraught as the German church appeared to be taken in by Nazi propaganda. And when the German Christian movement formed, in the 1930s, in order officially to support the incorporation of Nazi ideology into the mission and message of the church, and indeed to incorporate the church itself into the nationalist project of Hitler, both Barth and Bonhoeffer were ready to protest, to resist, to confess.

The opening salvo came from Barth in a monograph entitled *Theological Existence Today*, published in 1933. It was written in direct response to the numerous voices we have registered coming from the German Christian movement, all in a single chorus arguing that the coming of Adolf Hitler and the Nazis meant a revolutionary change for the whole direction of the church. Barth responded that, in such a time of politicized theology and church politics, the absolute requirement of faithfulness is "to carry on theology, and only theology, now as previously, as if nothing had happened."[6] Barth was not arguing for a quietist approach that simply ignored present circumstances; far from it. His point rather was that the basic orientation of theology does not shift, but pursues "the even tenor of its way even in the Third Reich."[7] Theology does not change its fundamental allegiance and direction, regardless of political development and pressure. He maintained this position knowing full well that, given the attitude of the German Christians, and especially the Nazis, it would amount to a profound protest of resistance, both in church politics and indirectly in politics as well. But no matter; we are called as teachers of theology, he argues, and we must remain true to our calling. And what is that calling? To be true to the Word of God; to make absolutely certain that "the Word be preached and heard," no matter the cost.[8] It is not the theologian, nor even the church, but the *Word of God* who triumphs over all opponents, for the Word is none other than the crucified, risen, and sovereign Lord, Jesus Christ,

6. Barth, *Theological Existence*, 9.
7. Ibid.
8. Ibid., 12.

who is "never to be found on our behalf save each day afresh in the Holy Scriptures of the Old and New Testaments."[9] To minister to this Word is the most pressing matter in every time, and especially in a time of crisis. Now, the great temptation of the age is to look away from the Word of God, and to seek guidance from another source, even in the church: "That is to say, we think ourselves capable of facing, solving and moulding definite problems better from some other source than that from and by means of God's Word."[10] To seek God's Word elsewhere than in Jesus Christ as found in the Scriptures is to cease to be the church, even in the name of some purported reform of the church. And that is exactly what the German Christians are doing, by turning to Nazism. At issue is the fundamental *vocation*, not only of the theologian, but of the church at large: "The special form of this temptation to us, the Church's preachers and teachers is, that possibly and actually there can be something like rivalry between our vocation within the Church and this or that other calling which is different . . . And thereby, the really first concern, and our particular vocation, become hopelessly lost . . . We are then no longer preachers and teachers of the Church."[11]

Barth saw three primary issues, which he hammers home in his rejection of German Christian teaching. First, he rejects the German Christian willingness to "coordinate" church life with Nazi policy as a necessary reform of the church. This is no reform at all, argues Barth, but sheer capitulation to political domination: "We ask, Did the decision for this purpose and action issue from the Church itself? Or, in other words, from the Word of God heard by this Church? *Or*, was it a suggestion not inwardly necessary, but one arising from political enthusiasm, or, perchance political scheming."[12] True reform of the church is always welcome; but what the German Christians offer is not reform of the church by

9. Ibid., 13.
10. Ibid., 15.
11. Ibid., 14.
12. Ibid., 22.

the *Word of God*, but fundamental alteration of the mission and message of the church in accordance with Nazi policy. The second spurious "reform" put in place by the German Christians in coordination with the Nazis was the invention of a new Reich Bishop, a single head of the entire Protestant church in Germany, where there had been none before. Why, Barth wonders, would the German Christians suddenly want such a figure in the present hour? "Mark the word!—they meant the principle of leadership as seen in the concrete form of Adolf Hitler and leaders under him. What other 'leader' could men be thinking about, when, in the Germany of the spring of 1933, the word was on men's lips?"[13] Keep in mind that the word for leader here is *führer*; the German Christians wanted a church führer in imitation of the great state führer, Adolf Hitler, and all the other little führers underneath him. It does not take any great insight, Barth argues, to recognize where this new "reform" is suddenly coming from; and it is not the Bible. Not even Luther and Calvin were given a special office, despite their obvious role in the church; Jesus Christ alone is the one head of the church. The third issue concerns the German Christian embrace of the Nazi principle of the *Volk*, and in particular the drive to make it impossible for non-Germans—that is, Jews who have converted to Christ—to be baptized members of the church. Barth responds, with little ambiguity: "What I have to say to all this is simply said. I say, absolutely and without reserve, NO! to both the spirit and the letter of this doctrine. I maintain that this teaching is alien, with no right, in the Evangelical Church. I maintain that the end of that Church will come if this teaching ever comes to have sway within her borders, as the 'German Christians' intend that it should."[14] The church of Jesus Christ has nothing to do with the racist Nazi principle of the *Volk*: "The church preaches the Gospel in all the kingdoms of this world. She preaches it also *in* the Third Reich, but not *under* it, not in *its* spirit."[15] Moreover, membership in the

13. Ibid., 35.
14. Ibid., 50.
15. Ibid., 52.

church is open to *all*: "The fellowship of those belonging to the Church is not determined by blood, therefore, not by race, but by the Holy Spirit and Baptism. If the German Evangelical Church excludes Jewish-Christians, or treats them as of a lower grade, she ceases to be a Christian Church."[16] Only baptism marks the true identity of the Christian, through the gift of the Holy Spirit; if *race* is introduced, there the church ceases to exist. Much of German Christian animus was directed against Barth and his influence in theology since the end of World War I; Barth, undeterred, made it crystal clear that it was not "his" theology at stake, not *any* particular theological movement, but the gospel itself as contained in Holy Scripture and treasured by the church.

Dietrich Bonhoeffer quickly offered his own response to Hitler and the German Christians. Characteristically it was shorter than Barth's, more focused, and perhaps for that very reason all the more powerful. While it can be quickly summarized, the impact is hard to overstate. It was Bonhoeffer who first raised the issue that would mold the Confessing Church into a focused effort. Bonhoeffer, above all, saw the Nazi persecution of the Jews, and the German Christian complicity in Nazi racism, as the key to church resistance. He writes in his essay "The Church and the Jewish Question" concerning state intervention in the life of the church, and church acquiescence in that intervention. The issue is the baptism of converted Jews, and the role of Jewish Christian pastors ordained by the church, both forbidden by the Aryan Clause of the Nazi state. With characteristic acuity, Bonhoeffer summarizes the issue facing both the church and the nation in 1933, upon Hitler's accession to power: "A state that threatens the proclamation of the Christian message negates itself."[17] For Bonhoeffer, a state that interferes with the legitimate function of the Christian church ceases to be a legitimate state; and that raises the question, what the church should do in this situation. He sees three options. The first option is to raise protest and resistance: "*first* . . . questioning the

16. Ibid.

17. Bonhoeffer, "The Church," in *Bonhoeffer Works* 12, 365.

state as to the legitimate state character of its actions, that is, making the state responsible for what it does."[18] Needless to say, in the totalitarian state of Nazi German that was hardly an easy prospect. The second option is to care for the victims of state violence: "The church has an unconditional obligation toward the victims of any societal order, even if they do not belong to the Christian community. 'Let us work for the good of all.'"[19] The third possibility, here left relatively undefined, is direct political action on the part of the church: "This is only possible and called for if the church sees the state to be failing in its function of creating law and order."[20] Bonhoeffer himself would come eventually to conclude that only the third option was enough, and would directly participate in the plot to assassinate Hitler. Regardless, says Bonhoeffer, one thing is clear: if the church capitulates concerning the issue of baptizing converted Jews, refusing to do so because of Nazi racist policy, the church ceases to be the church. Here Bonhoeffer makes the point that will lay the groundwork for the Confessing Church: "In such a case the church would find itself *in statu confessionis*."[21] It was Bonhoeffer who first raises the basic confessional issue: if the German Christians cross too many lines (and they do), then they cease to be the church. Nothing less than the truth of the gospel is at stake, and the only alternative is to *confess* the one faith of the gospel; that confession would of course become the Barmen Declaration.

We must leave Barth and Bonhoeffer for now, and turn directly to the Confessing Church and Barmen. But at least brief mention should be made on their subsequent fortunes. Barth was rarely shy; he in fact sent a copy of *Theological Existence Today* directly to Hitler with a very challenging personal message inscribed inside. The first edition sold out within a few weeks; the press printed copies as fast as it could, 37,000 in all, before it was banned by the Nazis just a few weeks after it appeared. Barth

---

18. Ibid.

19. Ibid. Quoting at the end Galatians 6:10.

20. Ibid., 366.

21. Ibid.

would soon be forced to leave Germany for Switzerland, where he taught dogmatics at Basel for the remainder of his life. The fate of Bonhoeffer is perhaps better known now, though at the time it was entirely unknown outside a very small circle of family and friends. He was deeply involved in ecumenical church affairs, not only in Germany but internationally. As suggested, he eventually came to the conclusion that only an attempt to assassinate Hitler could work, since obviously there would be no voting him out of office, and his crimes against humanity were growing daily, heinous beyond measure. The attempt failed, and Bonhoeffer was hanged, a martyr to Christ, in April of 1945.

Under the influence of Barth and Bonhoeffer, and in opposition to developments among the German Christians, the Confessing Church formed in 1934, and quickly summoned a national synod. It needs to be stressed again: the Confessing Church was always a small minority within the larger German church. While the numbers of the German Christians were never large either, their influence won the day; the German church at large eventually would follow Hitler. We do not record the deeds of the Confessing Church because they were stronger, but because they were right. The truth of their witness against Hitler, the Nazis, and the German Christian movement, is laid out with pristine theological clarity in the Barmen Declaration, formulated under the primary influence of Barth at a Synod of the Confessing Church in May of 1934. It should be added that the Barmen Declaration is not merely a historical monument to resistance; it is still a Confessing Document in many Christian denominations worldwide, including the United States.

A few points are helpful concerning what we can call the *logic of confessing*, points which hold true not only for the Barmen Declaration but for all creeds and confessions in the Christian church. The Barmen Declaration is not simply a statement of faith; that is, it is not trying to identify one set of beliefs (the Confessing Church) as over against another set of beliefs (the German Christians). As a true confession of the church of Jesus Christ, the Barmen Declaration is speaking the *one faith* of the gospel in a given situation. Statistically, that faith may be held and declared by only a minority, as it was indeed in Germany during this period; but in the logic of confession, that faith, as declared, is true nonetheless, and is uniquely true in that situation and moment, and true for all. Furthermore, the Barmen Declaration is speaking for the *whole church* of God in Jesus Christ, regardless of the statistical minority of its adherents. Though the issues may concern directly only Christians in Germany, the logic of confession requires that the whole church is in some sense present in the voice of those who declare the faith in that moment. As we will see, it is also not possible to *affirm* the faith without *denying the errors* that such a confession sets aside. Affirmation of faith in the logic of confession requires denunciation of error, traditionally called heresy, but in the Barmen Declaration called "false doctrine." Now, it is not enough that there are people in the church who may have some bad opinions about Christian faith; when is that not the case? We are all fallible. That alone does not require confession, and indeed not every period of the church necessitates the act of confessing. The need for confession arises when the errors become widespread, when they are accompanied by underhanded and heavily politicized tactics, and surrounded by an aura of misinformation and misdirection. In short, when widespread error is buttressed by a strategy of chaos and confusion, the act of confessing becomes necessary. Such an act, however, does not aim to *create* unity in the church; unity in the church already exists, for Jesus Christ himself is the true unity of the church. Confession aims rather to *preserve* the unity of the church against those—here the German Christians—who would shatter it by false teaching based on principles utterly alien to the witness of Scripture. Yet finally, the act of confessing makes no attempt to exclude from the church *people*, but rather false *teachings*. Christ alone is Lord of his church, and the Confession is ultimately laid before him as an act of repentance in a time of trial for all Christians.

There are six articles—called "truths"—in the Barmen Declaration, and each follows the same pattern. First, one or two scriptural verses are cited. Then, a theological confession is offered on the basis of those verses. And third, the errors of the German Christians relevant to that confession are then portrayed and rejected. The logic here is once again essential. The citation of Scripture comes first. The confession is only to be read in light of Scripture, and readers are challenged in the opening statements of the Barmen Declaration to look at the Scriptures, to test the contents. This is not a mere piece of traditional piety; Barth, Bonhoeffer, and the other leaders of the Confessing Church were deeply involved in Scriptural exegesis, and were firmly convinced that the German Christians had so far removed their teachings from Holy Scripture that the inner clarity of the divine Word would show itself without ambiguity to those willing to seek and to listen: "If you find that we are speaking contrary to Scripture, then do not listen to us! But if you find that we are taking our stand upon Scripture, then let no fear or temptation keep you from treading with us the path of faith and obedience to the word of God."[22] The six articles open with the following introduction: "In view of the errors of the 'German Christians' of the present Reich Church government which are devastating the church and are also thereby breaking up the unity of the German Evangelical Church, we confess the following evangelical truths."[23] There had been no such words, no such confession in Germany, since the time of the Reformation.

The first thesis begins with a verse from the Gospel of John: "I am the way, and the truth, and the life; no one comes to the Father, but by me"(John 14:6). Jesus Christ himself is speaking to his disciples; Jesus Christ, the living Subject, lays claim upon the whole of the church. The Bible is not a dead letter, but a living voice of the gospel; and the church even now hears in the Scriptures the crucified, risen, and exalted Lord say: I am myself alone the way. And so the verse is followed by the opening affirmation: "Jesus Christ, as he is attested for us in Holy Scripture, is the one Word of God which we have to hear and which we have to trust and obey in

---

22. Pelikan and Hotchkiss, eds., *Creeds and Confessions*, 507.

23. Ibid., 507.

life and in death."[24] It is certainly the most widely quoted thesis in the Barmen Declaration, and provides the theological framework for the whole. Recall that the basic background for the German Christian movement lay in the "theology of orders," the notion that outside of and prior to the Bible there was an "original revelation" from God that provided the true context for understanding the gospel. That original revelation is given in human experience, and affirms the basic structures of race, ethnicity, nationality, and so forth, in which people live. These structures provide the *context* in which the Scriptures, hence the gospel, are to be understood and interpreted. It was on the basis of this "original revelation," as we have seen, that the German Christians argued that the racial and nationalist propaganda of Hitler and the Nazis should be the true framework for the message of the church. The first thesis states the positive affirmation concerning the one genuine framework for church proclamation in word and deed: only Jesus Christ alone as he is attested in Holy Scripture is God's Word to the church and the world. We need to make a few points about this positive affirmation.

The opening thesis of the Barmen Declaration is not a kind of theological fundamentalism, as it is sometimes portrayed. To be sure, it binds the church to the direct, immediate, normative authority of Scripture; but that is hardly new. That has been the position of the mainstream church from the beginning, and remains the position of ecumenical Christianity. Yet the opening thesis makes it clear that Scripture itself is grounded in the absolute authority of the crucified, risen, and exalted Lord, Jesus Christ; he alone rules the church and the whole creation. It is by his authority alone that every word of Scripture is to be measured and understood. So, on the one hand, Scripture is not abstracted from its true content (the error of fundamentalism), which is Christ; yet on the other hand, Christ is not known apart from the one witness of Scripture (the error of religious liberalism, which Barth saw as the real theological background of the German Christian movement),

24. Ibid., 507.

which is the one true authority in the church. Notice: the Scripture, not the New Testament. The opening thesis makes it fully clear in its very affirmation that it will have nothing to do with the German Christian notion that the Old Testament is somehow foreign to the gospel. It is the *whole Bible*, in both Testaments, which points to Christ, the one true content of the Scriptures, God's Word to humanity. And it is to this authority that the *entire* church is bound. It is through Scripture alone that we hear the voice of the living Christ, are drawn to put our trust in him in every circumstance, to listen to his voice alone, and to obey him even unto death.

The negation that follows contains a fundamental rejection of the German Christian movement and the very theological foundation upon which it is based: "We reject the false doctrine, as though the church could and would have to acknowledge as a source of its proclamation, apart from and besides this one Word of God, still other events and powers, figures and truths, as God's revelation."[25] Having traced the teachings of the German Christians, we are in a position to understand just what this rejection is getting at. Recall the strident affirmations that Hitler was a miracle of God, sent by God to lead the German nation; recall the enthusiastic new discovery of the truths of race, ethnicity, nation, which now must guide the church in its understanding of its mission; recall the constant iteration of the new German church now being formed as a result of the Nazi seizure of power in 1933; and recall how *all* of these points were being used as fundamental truths guiding Christian teaching in a new direction; that is what Barmen is rejecting *in totality*. The point is not that these Christians are just a bit too animated about Hitler for their own good. The point rather is that, because of underlying *theological* errors, their enthusiasm for Hitler is resulting in a basic distortion of the gospel that is in fact no longer the Christian gospel, but false doctrine.

Having countered the very basis for German Christian theology in thesis one, and laid the foundation for a positive affirmation of the gospel in the Confessing Church, the Barmen Declaration

25. Ibid.

turns in thesis two to the basic foundation for Christian ethics in the broadest sense. What does it mean to serve and obey God in the church and the world in the time in which we live? The biblical quotation is from 1 Corinthians: "Christ Jesus, whom God made our wisdom, our righteousness and sanctification and redemption"(1 Cor 1:30). The church in Corinth was proud of its ability to find wisdom in a variety of sources, though it was willing to *incorporate* the new Christian message into its larger worldview. The Apostle Paul utterly rejects such an approach, indeed reverses it. There is no Christian *worldview*; there is only Christ. He not only defines the terms we use of him; in his person, he *constitutes* the relation we are freely given to God (justification), and the call we are given to serve others (sanctification). Christ is both gift and demand; the two can neither be collapsed nor separated. This leads, first, to the theological affirmation of the second thesis: "As Jesus Christ is God's assurance of the forgiveness of all our sins, so in the same way and with the same seriousness is he also God's mighty claim upon our whole life. Through him befalls us a joyful deliverance from the godless fetters of this world for a free, grateful, service to his creatures."[26] As we briefly expound this affirmation it should be noted: nowhere in the Barmen Declaration is the presence of Dietrich Bonhoeffer more clearly felt, though he was absent from the Synod. Thesis two is in many ways a brief exposition of *The Cost of Discipleship*, Bonhoeffer's early masterpiece.

What is the thesis affirming? The whole of our existence unfolds under the gracious will of God in Jesus Christ. As we trust him, so we must also obey him; as we obey him, so we must also trust him. The Word of God in Jesus Christ comes first as the free forgiveness of sins, justification by grace through faith alone. Nothing we have, nothing we do, contributes to our being in right relation to God. It is gift, pure and free, through the mercy of God in Jesus Christ, which comes to us through the forgiveness of all our sins. Yet we are not forgiven to live lives of sinful self-centeredness; just the opposite. The cross of Jesus Christ destroys

26. Ibid.

the power of sin, and claims our whole existence for a new life of service to God. It is not a burdensome service, given reluctantly or with hesitation, but a free and joyful service, given with gratitude for the bountiful mercy of God. Our redemption then is just this whole claim upon our lives, which comes in gift and demand, which is rendered in trust and obedience, which is not a principle or worldview but the living person of Jesus Christ himself. He is our wisdom; we know no ultimate truth worth knowing outside of him. And what, more exactly, is the new direction in life which the claim of Christ makes upon us? It is twofold. First, we are delivered *from* the godless fetters of this world. We will return to spell out the meaning of this more clearly in what the thesis rejects; but it is clear from our consideration of German Christian teaching that it is a direct attack on the idea that God has a special message to give us through the German people and nation, including its leaders. Such an idea is not true freedom, but bondage, slavery, from which the gospel sets us free. Second, we are set free *for* a free and grateful service to all God's creatures. Again, notice the clear affirmation: we are joined to *all* God's creatures, not just our fellow Germans, or our fellow Aryans, or even our fellow Christians. Blood and soil do not restrict or restrain God's love, neither can they restrict or restrain his command of love to us; we are bound in love and mercy to all. Moreover, our love for all is free and joyful, not coerced and perfunctory. We live out the claim of God upon our lives in love for all his creatures precisely because we are joined with them under the free forgiveness of sins; for all have sinned, and all have received his mercy. Every human being we meet is a creature of God beloved by Jesus Christ; that is our ethics.

Jesus Christ is God's promise of free forgiveness for all humanity; Jesus Christ is God's claim of love for all humanity; the necessary rejection of false doctrine based on these affirmations follows with comprehensive urgency: "We reject the false doctrine, as though there were areas of life in which we would not belong to Jesus Christ, but to other lords—areas in which we would not need justification and sanctification through him."[27] Behind the German Christian distortion of the gospel is an understanding of the *autonomy* of the various spheres of life. Among those are the church, the state, the economy, leisure, and of course race and ethnicity. The German Christian version of the gospel holds that the message of Jesus Christ is relevant to the concerns of the *church*, but that is as far as it goes. The various other dimensions of life have their own inner laws which operate according to their own inner dynamics. So, race is race; nation is nation; the führer is the führer; the church has no business interfering in these other realms. And of course this is exactly what Hitler and the Nazis wanted to hear. As long as the church kept safe within the bounds of clerical hocus pocus, Hitler was free to operate without criticism from the Christian community, and that by and large he did—except for the Confessing Church. For, according to the Barmen Declaration, *every* sphere of life—including the state—is under the rule of Christ. Every area of life *already* belongs to him, and not to other would-be lords. Every area of life has need of his *forgiveness*, certainly the church, but also the state and all its leaders, for they too are fallible. Every area of life has need of his mighty *claim* of love, including the state and its leaders, for they too are responsible ultimately to him, whether they realize it or not. Now, it is crucial to recognize, as we will see in the unfolding theses, that the Barmen Declaration is *not* here arguing for a Christian state, or even for Christian interference in the state, nor for a Christian party in German politics. It is rather simply arguing two points, both essential in the face of Nazi ideology. Everywhere Christians go, even into the public sphere, they carry with them both the gospel of forgiveness and the claim of love. They can no more leave that behind than they can leave their very identity; for Christ *is* their new identity. And second, whether Christians are present or not, Jesus Christ himself already rules all spheres of life in all nations of the earth. No sphere of life, and no person, is outside the scope of his rule. His rule is not a goal to be striven for, but a *universal*

27. Ibid.

reality now hidden, to be manifested in joyful love and service. To worship Christ in the church, and to follow Hitler in the state into the godless racism of Nazism, is for the Christian community, ontologically impossible.

The German Christians, and with them the vast majority of the church in Germany, had come to forget a most basic lesson of Christian discipleship: what it means to *be the church of Jesus Christ*. That was the conviction of the Confessing Church, and they sought to set out their reasons in the third thesis. It begins, as always, with a biblical quotation: "Rather, speaking the truth in love, we are to grow up in every way into him who is the head, into Christ, from whom the whole body is joined and knit together" (Eph 4:15–16). The church is the body of Christ; Christ is the one head of the church. Under him, through him, with him, the church is bound together as a living community of love and truth, joined together as one. Based on this biblical insight, the Barmen Declaration in the third thesis tackles the basic issue of the doctrine of the church. It does so, recall, in a situation in which the German Christians did not see the new totalitarian state of Hitler and the Nazis as an enemy, nor as neutral, but as a fundamental *friend* of the church, to which the church should be conformed, and under whose aegis the church should find solace and comfort. Such a church—utterly weak and cowardly in the face of Nazi evil—is no longer the church. So what does it mean to be the church in such a time of challenge?

We quote first in full: "The Christian Church is the congregation of the brethren in which Jesus Christ acts presently as the Lord in Word and Sacrament through the Holy Spirit. As the church of pardoned sinners, it has to testify in the midst of the sinful world, with its faith as with its obedience, with its message as with its order, that it is solely his property, and that it lives and wants to live solely from his comfort and from his direction in the expectation of his appearance."[28] It is essential to make fully clear, in confession, teaching, church order, and life together, that the

28. Ibid.

church belongs to Jesus Christ, and to him alone. The gospel of Jesus Christ utterly excludes all other lords; there is one Lord, one faith, one church gathered around and under him, the risen and exalted Lord, Jesus Christ. The church need not seek help from any other source; it seeks help only from the living and ruling Christ himself, who is actively *present* in the life of the church. The church is formed around the Easter faith; that Christ is risen, and even now lives and abides with his sisters and brothers. He sends them his Spirit, which is the very presence of the risen Lord not only with them, but among them and within their hearts, pervading their very existence. And the Spirit uses definite means to guide and teach the church: which are the Word and Sacrament. Without the Spirit, the Word and Sacrament are empty; but without Word and Sacrament, the Spirit is easily confused with the spirit of the age, which is not the living Spirit of Jesus Christ, the one head of the church. The risen Christ calls his people to live together in community, indeed as a family of faith, as sisters and brothers. There is one head, Christ; all others are bound together in love under him. There are no "leadership principles" floating through the life of the church, despite the need for good order. Love brings growth; growth fosters new love. The church is composed of forgiven sinners, and speaks to a world of sinners the one message of forgiveness. There is here, and can be here, nothing of strong vs. weak, racially superior vs. racially inferior; all such markers of inhumanity are not only alien to the gospel, but radically rejected. *All humanity* is defined simply before God in terms of the free promise of the forgiveness of sins. Even in love, the gathered church are still sinners; precisely out of love, the church takes the gospel of forgiveness to all in the world, sinners alike. Christ alone rules every dimension of the church's life, and that includes its order. Here is Barmen's rejection of the Aryan Clause. The Nazi state has no right to tell the church who it can baptize, or who can be its ordained clergy. The German Christians had capitulated to Nazi racism; the Confessing Church professes Christ alone as the foundation for the order of the church: Christ Jesus the Jew of Nazareth, who gathers into one all peoples and nations of the earth. The mission of the church is to proclaim him, and him alone; the one hope of the church is the return of Christ, and it looks to him, and only to him.

The rejection of the false doctrine of the German Christians is once again both forceful and precise: "We reject the false doctrine, as though the church were permitted to abandon the form of its message and order to its own pleasure or to changes in prevailing ideological and political convictions."[29] The German Christians had been seduced by Hitler and the Nazis. They thought they could *add* National Socialist teaching to Christian truth in order to make it more relevant. What happened of course is that Christian truth was lost, and National Socialist teaching took over. Their message became a corrupt vision of strength though self-improvement, not the free forgiveness of sins through grace alone. Their order became a reflection of Nazi racism, not a mirror of divine love. They thought they were adapting the gospel to Nazi philosophy in a way that preserved the essential elements of both. In fact, they inevitably adopted Nazism, and abandoned the essence of Christian truth. They put their hope in a thousand-year Reich; but God's coming kingdom is eternal, and a thousand years in his sight are as nothing, as dust that the wind forever blows away.

The fourth thesis once again directly attacks an error of the German Christians, yet in such a way as to gain greater insight into the truth of Scripture for the contemporary world. The German Christians fully adopted the führer principle into the life of the church. That is, they taught that the offices of the church should be understood in terms of *obedience to authority*, and sought to institute a single Reich Bishop who would have ultimate authority over the entire German Protestant Church. From top to bottom, the church was to be ruled in the same manner as the Nazi State. The fourth thesis cites a passage from the Gospel of Matthew, in which Jesus is speaking to the disciples: "You know that the rulers of the Gentiles lord it over them, and their great exercise authority over them. It shall not be so among you; but whoever would

29. Ibid.

be great among you must be your servant" (Matt 20:25–26). Jesus here turns the world of human political rule—including that of the Roman Empire—upside down. In the new light of Christ, true authority is not defined as *power over* others, but as *service toward* them. Such service is not *less than* the power of worldly princes, but ultimately far greater, infinitely greater; for it is offered freely in love. Notice: this is not substituting one ideology for another; not putting an ideology of servile subservience in place of overbearing lordship. That would simply be to flip the same coin to the other side. The issue is ultimately *christological*; in the community of faith, Jesus Christ himself is the true pattern of life, and in free service to others he exercised his true Lordship over all. *He* is the pattern, not an ideology, or worldview. And so the thesis affirms: "The various offices in the church do not establish a dominion of some over the others; on the contrary, they are for the exercise of the ministry entrusted to and enjoined upon the whole congregation."[30] What is at issue?

First, it is vital to point out the phrase "various offices." The Barmen Declaration makes no determination concerning the extent and nature of church offices. That is, it applies to churches that have bishops, or presbyteries, or are simply organized congregationally, and so forth. As important as the question of church offices may be, the broader question of true service in the church is at issue. To exercise authority in the church is to serve, in conformity to Christ; it is not to dominate. However such offices are understood in this or that church polity, there can be no question in the church of Jesus Christ of rank, or privilege; only of excellence in service and love. Service of God in Christ; service of one another; service of humanity; these are the forms of Christian life in the community of faith, which must at times be set *over against* the culture of the world, when it finds itself held captive to an ideology of dominion. Second, such service, paradoxically, is true freedom. Dominion is a form of bondage; the ruler is ultimately bound to the good opinion of the ruled, while the ruled are bound

30. Ibid., 508.

to the good graces of the ruler. Only service of the other is truly free, in the paradox of grace. I am only perfectly free when I serve; I truly serve others, not when I am under begrudging obligation or misguided subservience, but only when I am set truly free by the gospel of Jesus Christ. And third, every exercise of any office in the church—one thinks of the minister of the Word, the singer in the choir, the keeper of the finances, the mower of the church lawn—every exercise of any office is a work of the *whole* church. We all have different gifts, but the same Spirit inspires them all for the common good, and therefore no service in the church is the act of an isolated individual, but ultimately a delegated act of the whole community of faith.

There is of course here a profound protest, and it comes out in the rejection: "We reject the false doctrine, as though the church, apart from this ministry, could and were permitted to give to itself, or allow itself to be given to it, special leaders vested with ruling powers."[31] The word for leaders in this passage is of course *Führern*. When the German Christians proclaimed: One Reich, One Church, One Führer!, they were not only pledging their subservience to Hitler, but introducing into the church the principle of leadership of the Nazi state. And that principle was rule, and be ruled: the rule of the few, the subservience of the many. The German Christians saw themselves as a special ruling elite within the church, invested with powers to guide the church in the same way that the Nazis were guiding the nation. The Barmen Declaration is quite clear: there is not now, nor is there ever, a special *ruling elite* *i*n the church of Jesus Christ. There are always various offices, to be sure; there is authority in the church. But such authority is *in* the church, not *over* the church; and it is patterned after the one true Lord, who rules by serving.

Thesis five opens with a short biblical quote: "Fear God. Honor the Emperor" (1 Pet 2:17). Both as it occurs in the context of the Scripture, and as a citation of the Bible in the Barmen Declaration, the short text conceals a profound truth, which relates

31. Ibid.

to the basic issue of *church and state*. It is the Word of God which declares our mutual relation to both; in both the sphere of the church, and in the sphere of the state, we are under the Word of God. As Christians, says Peter, we have an obligation, a responsibility, to both, declared and determined by the Word. But it is different. We *fear* only God. Only God deserves our ultimate trust, our ultimate obedience, our ultimate love. We cannot and must not transfer that trust and obedience and love to any other: "we must obey God rather than any human authority," as Peter declares in the book of Acts, when challenged to obey an earthly ruler by disobeying God (Acts 5:29). Nevertheless, the state has its own proper claim upon the Christian community, under the declaration of the divine word. We *honor* the Emperor. We do not fear the state; but we do honor its claim upon human life. It is under God, and therefore not free from just criticism, even from the church; but it is to be fully respected, not as an abstract authority, but as a servant of God's own will and word. On the basis of this biblical text, the Barmen Declaration offers its thesis: "Scripture tells us that, in the as yet unredeemed world in which the church also exists, the State has by divine appointment the task of providing for peace and justice. It fulfills this task by means of the threat of force, according to the measure of human judgment and ability. The church acknowledges the benefit of this divine appointment in gratitude and reverence before him. It calls to mind the Kingdom of God, God's commandment and righteousness, and thereby the responsibility both of rulers and of the ruled. It trusts and obeys the power of the Word by which God upholds all things."[32] Let us briefly unpack this extraordinary statement.

Both the church and the state live in a world in which divine redemption through the cross and resurrection of Jesus Christ is as yet not fully consummated. We are all fallible, both as members of the church and as citizens in the state. Yet in this fallible world, God has not only instituted his church by the power of the Word, he has likewise appointed the state to its own very different role.

32. Ibid.

Both church and state stand under the divine rule in Jesus Christ; yet each has a different role to play. The role of the state—its task as defined, not by the church, or by the state itself, but by the Word of God—is to provide for the peace and justice of humankind. These are biblical words: peace is life together in friendship not only within a state, but between states; justice means the promotion and protection of the common good of all. Indeed, in the Bible, the concepts are paired; there can be no peace without justice, just as there can be no true justice without peace; and it is the task of the state to promote both together. When there are those who would violate the norms of peace and justice, the state can coerce assent on the part of citizens. But it does not have that power infallibly; the state too has only human judgment, and human ability, and is therefore always open to criticism and correction. Nevertheless, while fallible, the state is a divine gift for which the church too is grateful. God's own realm is echoed in the mutual obligations of governor and governed in the state. Once again, however, it is to God alone, not the state, to whom the church looks, in trust and obedience, for God's own Word infinitely transcends every human power. In short, Christians are to act responsibly in the state, but their *allegiance* is under no circumstances to become *submission*.

The thesis then offers two rejections, in essence of the same error, but coming from opposite directions. The first statement reads: "We reject the false doctrine, as though the State, over and beyond its special commission, should and could become the single and totalitarian order of human life, thus fulfilling the church's vocation as well."[33] Notice, this is false doctrine; that is, it is being taught by the *church*. The German Christians themselves were teaching that the State, through its concepts of family, blood, soil, and race, had the right to delimit the message and mission of the church. The church could preach inner piety, but should leave such broader national direction to definition by the state. The Barmen Declaration simply says no. When the church allows its mission and message to be defined by claims laid upon it by State slogans

33. Ibid.

and buzzwords, it is no longer the church. The other error comes to the same end, but from the opposite direction: "We reject the false doctrine, as though the church, over and beyond its special commission, should and could appropriate the characteristics, the tasks, and the dignity of the State, thus itself becoming an organ of the State."[34] Once again this is false teaching *by the church*. The German Christians wanted to see themselves as a part of the new Nazi order that Hitler was creating. They wanted to coordinate the life of the church with the new Third Reich, in such a way that the church would live within, not apart from, the Reich. That is, they took on a second task alongside their one true commission of preaching and teaching the divine Word and administering the divine Sacraments through the power of the Holy Spirit; and that was to become a *cheerleader* for the State. Inevitably, their message began to mirror the State, not the divine Word, and they ceased to be the church.

The final thesis of the Barmen Declaration is, in many ways, a resounding affirmation of the basic point at issue that not only separates the German Christians from the Confessing Church, but from the universal church of all times and places. That issue is the call of Christ to the mission of the church. The biblical text is from the so-called Great Commission, which I will quote here in full: "Go therefore and make disciples of all nations, baptizing them in the name of the Father and of the Son and of the Holy Spirit, and teaching them to obey everything that I have commanded you. And remember, I am with you always, to the end of the age" (Matt 28:19–20). The risen Christ gathers with his disciples, and sends them out in mission to all peoples and all nations of the earth. There is now no restriction; he is the exalted Lord, with authority over all creation. Their mission in service to the word of the gospel is therefore unlimited in scope. The power that guides, renews, and directs their mission is the presence of Jesus Christ himself. The promise of his presence is the one true link between his call to mission and the unfolding witness of the disciples among all

34. Ibid.

peoples. Recall now the German Christian view: that the church in Germany has the mission of building up the German race, the German *Volk*, the German people. All aspects of church life, on their view, are to be coordinated toward this end: that the new revival of German life under Hitler and the Nazis is served by the German church, for that is what national mission entails. German Christianity is Germanic, special to the German people and nation; the mission of the church in *Germany* is therefore to aid the Germanic nature of both church and society. We will quote the rejection first, and then end this chapter with the affirmation: "We reject the false doctrine, as though the church in human arrogance could place the Word and work of the Lord in the service of any arbitrarily chosen desires, purposes, and plans."[35] Mission is the *Lord's* Word, the *Lord's* work; it unfolds under *his* promise, and is undertaken only through *his* commission. We are witnesses, servants, of the Word; to arbitrarily design our own mission, in contradiction to the biblical word and promise, is the height of human arrogance and folly. Such a redefined, nationalist, human mission will fail in the end, for it is not upheld by the promise of the risen Lord, Jesus Christ.

So what, then, is the true mission of the church? If anything, we end directly at the heart of the matter between the Confessing Church and the German Christians: "The church's commission, upon which its freedom is founded, consists in delivering the message of the free grace of God to all people in Christ's stead, and therefore in the ministry of his own Word and work through sermon and Sacrament."[36] The church *cannot* and *must not* choose its mission; it is given its mission by *commission*, through the Risen Christ. He alone is the source of the mission of the church, beside whom there is no other. But serving this Lord, unlike the false lords of this world, is not blind submissive subservience, but true freedom. The *authority* of Christ over the church is the one ground for authentic freedom *within* the church. Why is this so? Because

35. Ibid.
36. Ibid.

Christ himself is the gift of God's free grace, who binds us to himself in love, and calls us to go forth with that same free grace into the world. It happens as the church gathers for worship; every act of worship is at the same time an act of mission. The church gathers to hear the sermon preached, and to celebrate the Sacrament of the Lord's Supper. They gather because the risen Christ himself gathers them; and the same risen Christ sends them out into the world. The life of the community of faith is not self-grounded; it is always newly open to the direction of Christ through his promised presence. He is risen; the church is now his body, his voice, his messengers in the world. Where they speak, he speaks; where they act, he acts. In word and deed, they are his witnesses, and he lives through them.

So what is the message of the church to the world? It is on this issue that the Barmen Declaration strikes down the whole structure of the German Christian movement, and with it the ideology of Hitler and Nazi Germany. God's Word, the gospel, is God's *free grace*. We are not put right with God because we are German, or Aryan, or any race or nation or ethnicity. God's grace exposes the utter sinfulness of every such attempt to erect human standing before God and in the world on the basis of human categories of achievement and ability, of whatever sort. Only God's grace alone puts us right with God; and that message is given to the church to be proclaimed *to all people* (*an alles Volk*). Not the German *Volk* only; not the healthy as opposed to the weak; not the Aryan as opposed to the Jew or the Slav; not the "normal" as opposed to the "degenerate"; but *to all people*. In the stead of Christ himself, the church in service of the gospel breaks down every single barrier erected by human beings. Why? Not because the church has some special insight into human anthropology. No, *God himself* has already torn down every such barrier through the cross of Jesus Christ. The grace of the gospel is free to all; the mission of the church therefore reaches out to all, no matter what barriers it must cross. Ultimately, the mission of the church grounded in the promise of the risen Christ shatters the German Christian ideology, and the Nazi barbarism upon which it is based.

PART II

~~~

Our Church Struggle

In the case of Hitler and National Socialism in Germany, the man and the movement were inseparable. There are numerous reasons why this was the case, many going back to the origins of Nazism and the development of the führer principle. After the Enabling Acts of 1934, in which Germany became a Nazi dictatorship, it was fully clear that Adolf Hitler would rule for life. He could not be voted out of office. At that point, the destiny of Nazism, and the destiny of Hitler the person, became identified, as Hitler himself in his raging narcissism always believed them to be. Indeed, he was angry when diplomacy deprived him of war in 1938, so eager was he to start the wars of conquest leading to growth in *Lebensraum* before he grew too old. At his death by suicide, German Nazism ceased to exist as a world-historical force, though of course fascism continues as a threat in many places, including Germany itself.

With Donald Trump it is different. The man and the movement are obviously intertwined, even codependent. Nevertheless, they can and must be distinguished. Trumpism is clearly in many respects an echo of the personality and views of Donald Trump.

However, he will someday no longer be in office, either by being voted out, or serving out his final term. It is entirely conceivable in American democracy that another will take up the mantle of Trumpism, and the movement will continue even after the man is no longer in office to lead it. We will thus first briefly sketch the personality of Donald Trump, and then the movement he has spawned.

Once again, in the case of Hitler, there is little need to guess at his aims and personality; his book *Mein Kampf* expressed them publicly in grandiose horror. For those who had eyes to see, he was an open book. Donald Trump's own personal *Mein Kampf* is just as open, just as clear; but it is not written in a single book. Trump is not a book person; he is a creature of television, with episodes and seasons, cliffhangers and drama. His life is being displayed serially, as it were, in daily and weekly tweets, tens of thousands of them, often several a day, even several an hour. Like Hitler he is not hiding from anyone. One only has to read—in noxious horror—to take the measure of the man.

Trump is endlessly, boundlessly, obsessed with the sheer grandeur that is he, himself. He has the highest IQ; he has the most beautiful house; he is the smartest person there is; he has the most beautiful everything. He is smarter than the generals, smarter than the politicians, smarter than the economists, and for that matter better educated than everyone else. He has the biggest crowds; the best hotels; the best golf course; the best fragrances. He is the only person alive who can fix the problems of the country: jobs, relations with Israel, national security, healthcare, immigration, tax laws, infrastructure. One thing he will not have to fix is global warming, because it is all a big hoax, a mythical, fictional con job; he knows this because he is smarter than the stupid scientists. He is by far the least racist person who ever lived, and has done more for people with disabilities than anyone else, ever. No one respects women more than Donald Trump. It is just sad, so sad, that not everyone can be like him.

If nothing else, Donald Trump has made a vast and permanent contribution to the vocabulary of incessant, brutal, demeaning, dehumanizing hate. His lexicon of hate is, by his own admission, not merely occasional, but a way of life. Often his words of hate are couched in mental health terms: people are nutjobs, wacko, basket cases, psycho, stupid, average, dumb, a disaster. His disdain for the news media is open to see: they are shoddy, liars, biased, lazy, stupid, terrible, garbage, failing, dummies, clowns, low IQ, underachieving, third rate, a total joke, the worst, a laughingstock, lightweight, crazy, doomed. He does not rest with calling someone a clown, nor even a stupid clown; he must call them a *really stupid* clown for it to reach the level of disdain for others he means to convey. At least his hate does not keep him from public duties; he regularly extends holiday good wishes to all Americans, even the haters and the losers. He has a special vocabulary of hate reserved for women, focusing on their body parts, their looks, or comparing them to certain animals. Women are described as horseface, fat, ugly, bleeding, pig, disgusting, crazed, crying, lowlife, nasty, extremely unattractive. This is of course not locker room talk; this is misogyny, the cruel, vicious, and systematic degrading of women. In fact, Trump has been accused by numerous women of sexual assault, and notoriously has bragged, in conversations caught on tape, about unwanted and aggressive actions toward women that include sexual assault.

And finally, there are the lies, repeated, endlessly disgorged, thrust out into the civil body politic like presidential projectiles. Muslims openly celebrating the attacks on the World Trade Center in New Jersey; knowing nothing of David Duke and the Ku Klux Klan; the size of the crowd on Inauguration Day; winning the most electoral votes since Ronald Reagan; people being bussed across state lines to vote; historic delays for cabinet nominations (despite the fact that the historic delays for nominations in all levels of the executive branch are his own); that the murder rate is the highest in forty-five years; lies about voter fraud; lies about golf; lies about daily duties; the list is nearly endless, and continues to grow with each passing day of his presidency. He lies, and then he lies about the lies. Perhaps the only good thing that can be said about the astounding capacity of Donald Trump for lying is that he has created many new jobs for all those journalists who must now regularly keep tabs on all his lies. Journalists he then lies about even more.

Personal grandiloquent grandiosity; paranoid and persistent hatreds; incessant lying; that is the *person* of Donald Trump, writ large in daily tweets for the whole nation, the whole world to see. There is no guesswork involved. We are not interpreting Trump; he is announcing himself. We are merely observing the person he chooses to be. Now, what is the governing political philosophy that is generated by, and coheres with, the person? It is hardly a surprise that the pathologies and hatreds of the person are expressed in the politics. We can here offer only a brief summary, in order to focus on the evangelical *reasons* for supporting that philosophy of politics, and the policies that it produces.

For Donald Trump, the entire world is divided up into two categories: the strong and the weak. These are, for him, moral categories. To be strong is to be good; to be weak is to be bad, a loser, sad, disgusting. The moral axis of strength and weakness in fact turns on the person of Trump himself. He is strength, and those who agree with him are the strong. All who oppose him in any way are the weak. All other defining characteristics are irrelevant. POWs are weak, insofar as they oppose Trump; parents of children lost in combat are weak, because they do not stand by Trump; paraplegics are weak, because they criticize Trump. The weak become strong the moment they change and support Trump; the strong become weak the instant they veer from total allegiance to Trump. Trump does not merely embody strength; he defines it. Whatever he is and does *is* strength; whatever he opposes *is*, by its very nature, weak. Strength and weakness, good and evil, are defined in reference to Donald Trump, as his overflowing Twitter account so eloquently attests.

Yet we must probe one level deeper. We are not discussing what *is*; we are discussing what *appears* to be. Hitler was obsessed with what he considered a real, though obviously demented, notion of biological anarchy. For Trump, the battle between strength and weakness, which is the same as the battle between good and evil, revolves around the *appearance* of things. If it is *seen* to be strong, it is strong; if it *seen* to be weak, it is weak. Trump evinces no conception of *actual* strength or weakness, but only the public *perception*. He is obsessed with image, with brand, with celebrity, with status. The battle that rages in the world of Trump is not social Darwinism, but socialite Darwinism. Trump's very words define reality; if he says it is lawful, it is lawful. If he says things are fine, things truly are fine. If he says things are a disaster, then things are in fact a disaster. Those who disagree are losers, sad, weak.

With the moral categories of the strong and the weak as the fundamental conception, we quickly rehearse the basics of Trumpism. America is in sharp decline (for reasons we will discuss below); it must be made strong, great again. Only Donald Trump can make this happen through the sheer force of his will. He inherited a national hellscape; he will make a great nation again. He will do so by measuring every decision by the truth that *national self-interest* is the highest moral truth in world affairs. Loyalty to country; loyalty to each other, who share the same blood; total allegiance to the nation—this loyalty will bring about renewal. Strength, safety, pride, greatness—these all come from knowing this one great truth: that national self-interest is the one true measure of right and wrong in world affairs. Trump himself will decide what is in the American national self-interest, for he alone can do so in this great hour of decision and action.

Nations are tied together by blood, by a sovereign will, by pride and confidence in shared values and ways of life. America in particular is blessed by God. Anyone who rejects these truths cannot and must not be accepted. To disagree with these truths is not only unacceptable; it makes one an enemy of the state, an enemy of America. Some enemies are clearly *inside* the borders of the nation, and they are especially members of the press, and members of the opposition party, the Democrats. They are weak, they are losers, they are enemies of America, they are enemies of the people. But other enemies are *outside* the state, and the worst of those are immigrants and refugees, especially from Latin America and the Middle East. From such places come only murderers, rapists, terrorists, drug dealers. Immigration from the Middle East and Latin America has to be stopped. A wall has to be built along the entire southern border to keep the enemies out. Mexico must pay for it, for they send the dregs of their society to plague our nation, destroy our values, and weaken our national will.

In short, all policies, whether healthcare, climate change, immigration, tax codes, and so forth, must be determined in the light of a life-or-death struggle between the weak and the strong. America has been *weakened*; again, we will discuss why shortly. But under Donald Trump it will be *strengthened*, not so much because of any particular ideas or policies, but because he is now the President and others are not. He is himself the source of strength for the nation. Therefore, what is good for *him*, is good for the nation. What honors *him*, honors the nation. By contrast, what *criticizes* him, attacks America. Whoever would *question* him, is betraying the people. He is not only identical to the office he holds; he is identical to the national good, which is inseparable from his own well-being and good fortune. There is one heart, one home, one destiny, one country, and one true source of all national strength: Donald Trump.

3

Evangelicalism and the Politics
of Trumpism

Evangelicalism has wholeheartedly embraced not only the man
Donald Trump, but the politics of Trumpism as well. Our
aim in this chapter is to profile the nature of that embrace, and to
examine the reasons for it, using whenever possible words taken
from evangelical voices themselves.

But first some background. We saw that the immediate background to the rise of the German Christian movement was the
unsettling democracy of the Weimar Republic; while the very different background to the rise of the Confessing Church was the
cataclysm of World War I. We begin by asking: what provides the
most prominent background, which helps to explain why evangelicalism so completely and absolutely embraced Trump and his
political philosophy? The answer is not difficult. it was the election of the first black man as president of the United States, Barack
Hussein Obama.

It was Trump himself who led the way in the attacks on
Obama. His treatment of Obama was vicious, personal, brutal, and
utterly fallacious in every respect. If Trump did not begin the long
string of lies and hatreds that would extend into his presidency by

his attacks on President Obama, he certainly used them to solidify his paranoid, conspiratorial style. Obama is horrible, incompetent, has no understanding, is a total disaster, a terrible executive, a pathetic excuse, a delusional failure, the worst president ever, fawning and desperate, pathetic, totally stupid, totally incompetent, thick, irrational, just plain incompetent. The string of hateful tirades is of course much longer, but one gets the point; one also quickly realizes we are learning about Trump, not about Obama.

Donald Trump continued his attacks on President Obama by fostering the so-called birther controversy, an overtly racist attempt to demean and delegitimize the first African American president of the United States. According to Trump, all presidents are required to *show* their birth certificates to prove that they are American citizens. Where is Obama's, he asks, in the language of far-right conspiracy theory. Trump claimed to send investigators who could find no doctors or nurses who remembered attending Obama's birth; claimed that Obama was spending millions of dollars defending the issue, trying desperately to make it go away. It was of course all an empty hoax, a swindle, a con, a lie. But it was not only Trump who found it difficult, even impossible, to accept the election of the first black president of the United States, regardless of his obvious qualifications and accomplishments; evangelicals joined him in this noble and righteous cause.

I do not think it accurate to say that the election of the first black president of the United States *changed* evangelicalism; it was already set along its way. But I think that it *hardened* evangelicalism, especially its worst instincts, leading it down a path that could only end in theological disaster. Evangelicals leaders launched a series of vicious attacks on Obama in the run-up to 2008, and predicted that if elected he would bring unmitigated disaster to—or rather upon—the United States. Boys Scouts of America would cease to exist; private Christian schools would be closed, and Christian teachers would be fired from public schools; there would be no hospital access for people over eighty; Iran would detonate a nuclear bomb in Tel Aviv; conservative radio talk shows would be shut down by the government, while Bush government officials would be imprisoned. These were among the predictions openly circulating among evangelicals, outdoing even Trump's vivid and paranoid imagination. If anything, the election of 2012 was even worse; it was called by evangelicals the most consequential election since 1860, a rather interesting and notable reference. Franklin Graham put it this way: "The President (Obama) is leading the nation on a sinful course, and God will judge him and us as a nation if we don't repent."[1] James Dobson was similarly measured; speaking of the family under Obama, he argued that it "will likely crumble, presaging the fall of Western Civilization."[2] Mike Huckabee called the Obama victory in 2012 a humiliating defeat and he called for national repentance. There was talk of global economic collapse, of the Antichrist, of pulling children out of public schools, buying farmland and guns, and awaiting the end. There was, as we shall discuss below, the inevitable spectre of the coming of a new world dictator. Many evangelicals were convinced by their leaders and pastors that Obama was not a Christian but a Muslim, despite the fact that he was (and is) a practicing Christian, well able not only to articulate but also to apply his faith to work and life. Word spread that he swore his oath of office on a copy of the Koran. The fact is, it is hard to overstate how quickly evangelical anger, fear, and hatred solidified so rapidly upon the election of the first black president. While a few leaders tried to mitigate it, most stoked it. Here is the summary by Wayne Grudem, a leading evangelical theologian, of the Obama presidency: "I look at my own nation, the United States of America, and I see signs of increased evil. I am concerned that God in heaven . . . might bring judgment on the nation for its evil, just as he has on other nations in the past—judgment in terms of economic collapse, an incurable disease epidemic, a military attack from powerful enemies, the imposition of a totalitarian government, or some other means."[3]

1. Fitzgerald, *The Evangelicals*, 619.

2. Ibid.

3. Grudem, *Politics*, 596.

Think about that; God will send utter ruin, death, destruction, and total collapse upon the United States, because they elected the first black man as president. As we will continue to see, both Trumpism and its evangelical support is in large measure designed not simply to counter the policies of Obama, but in their version of reality to *erase his existence* from history, to undo as it were his very election. If Obama was not an American, he could not be a Christian; if he was not a Christian, he could not be an American; and therefore, both from the perspective of Trumpism and evangelicalism, the legacy of Obama must simply be rooted out. Indeed, perhaps the election of 1860 is not such a bad metaphor after all.

We now begin our primary task: to understand how a Christian movement, evangelicalism, could embrace the person and politics of Donald Trump. We have seen that the German Christians could embrace Hitler based on their *theology of orders*. That is, they looked *backward*, behind the Bible, to a creation theology given in human experience by which the Bible and indeed all reality must be interpreted. Evangelicalism looks in the opposite direction, to the *endtime*, ahead of the Bible. For evangelicalism, prophetic experience of the endtime gives true insight not only into the genuine teachings of the Bible, but also into the true shape of current events, especially political events.

It is helpful to remember how mainstream Christianity has treated the same complex of issues, based on the canonical shape of the Bible. It is well known to readers of the Bible that especially the book of Daniel in the Old Testament, and the book of Revelation in the New Testament, contains a series of visions and images unlike any other part of canonical Scripture. These images and visions point to the endtime, termed *apocalyptic*; they use pictures of cosmic judgment, with hordes of enemies descending upon the people of God in final, pitched battle. The book of Revelation speaks of the persecution of the saints, the terrors of the great tribulation, the appearance of the Antichrist. Yet the book of Revelation sums up the entire apocalyptic tradition of the whole Bible with an astounding witness, whose inner logic has guided the mainstream church. The images of the apocalypse are to be understood in the light of the life, death, resurrection, and exaltation of Jesus Christ, and *not* the reverse. We do not start with the images and vision of the endtime, and fit the figure of Christ in along with other events; just the *opposite*. Only the present and exalted Lord, Jesus Christ, is the true norm for understanding the images and visions of the endtime. The book of Revelation leaves three conclusions, all embraced by ecumenical Christendom. First, from the perspective of heaven, the endtime lies already in the past. It is all accomplished! Christ has already defeated all enemies of the church: "Fallen, fallen is Babylon the great! It has become a dwelling place of demons, a haunt of every foul and hateful beast" (Rev 18:3). The great events of the endtime, when understood in the light of the cross, have *already been accomplished* through the almighty death and resurrection of Jesus Christ. It is finished! Yet second, the community of faith on earth continues from a time-bound perspective to experience genuine suffering and struggle, which is never denied. The victory of Christ, already accomplished, does not mitigate the depth of suffering, but serves rather to encourage the endurance of faith and love as God's eternity unfolds over time. The image of a future millennium is a reminder that eternity is not fixed, but as God's own time enters human life in stages. And third, there can be absolutely no basis for predicting the future based on the Bible. Christ himself strictly *forbids* it, and he is himself the truth to which the whole Scriptures point: "It is not for you to know the times or periods that the Father has set by his own authority" (Acts 1:6). In short, as the community of faith, the church awaits in patience and trust the return of Christ, watching and waiting upon him in service to others, confident and joyful even in times of deepest struggle. Such is the inner logic of the biblical witness as embraced by the mainstream of the Christian church; and on this basis, various attempts in the early church to chart the progress of the endtime were dismissed as the false teaching of chiliasm or millenarianism.

Evangelicalism has, from its inception in the nineteenth century, reversed the inner logic of Scripture. Rather than understanding apocalyptic images and language in the light of Jesus Christ, it has sought to lay out a precise *timeline* of the endtime based on the books of Daniel and Revelation (and portions of other books in the Bible), to be sure fitting Christ into the unfolding picture, but nonetheless mostly absorbed by the detailed timeline itself. Christ becomes just one more item in the evangelical version of the endtime, not the Lord of time who alone interprets all time. Evangelicalism itself purports to hold the true key—based on the Bible to be sure, but read *against* the inner logic of the biblical witness—to the unfolding events of the future. Issues of nationalism, race, immigration, and so forth, will all come to fit into this all-encompassing evangelical claim to know the true secret of the apocalypse, even including the role of Trump himself. We therefore need to explore the evangelical approach to endtime more closely, if only briefly.

Certain features of American evangelical apocalyptic have been apparent since its inception. Each new generation of evangelicals see its own time as the last days before the end. The end will not come easily, but with terrible violence and human tragedy. Yet the events of the day—each new generation makes the same claim—can be predicted from the ingredients of the Bible down to details. When the predictions fail, new predictions are put forward to explain the purported failure of the previous predictions. All predictions are predicated upon a cosmic battle between good and evil, in which only one side can win, and the other must lose. It is never predicted that America will lose; it is never predicted that America's enemies will win. It is always predicted that America will win; it is always predicted that America's enemies will lose. There is no middle ground; apocalyptic in the hands of evangelical prophesy is a zero-sum game in which one side must go home the ultimate winner, while the other side must go home the ultimate loser. All one has to do is read the newspaper (or, in the twentieth century listen to the radio, or watch television, or now check out the Internet) to confirm that the endtime is now here, right around the corner, and evangelicalism has unlocked the mystery of future prediction based on the Bible.

It is of course not to be overlooked that virtually all evangelical predictions dovetail rather exactly with the politics of the Republican Party. World War I was the final battle before the endtime, and the Democrat Wilson was the dupe of Satan leading the nation into Armageddon. After the war—when the world did not come to an end, though it certainly appeared to—the League of Nations turned out to be predicted in the Bible as the place where the Antichrist will descend and flourish, and the end will come. Then Al Smith, a Democratic grandson of Roman Catholic immigrants running for president, was seen as the last great tool of Satan, before the end. Billy Sunday declared that the labor movement was the final great sign of the end of days. FDR was despised by evangelical prophecy for his role in bringing about the end of time under the delusions of the devil, including his erection of the edifice of Social Security, a sure sign of the coming end. The Cold War of course brought the Soviet Union into the orbit of evangelical predictions of the end, along with the atomic bomb. This is the last generation, the word went out, yet again, and we have the biblical texts to prove it once and for all! Harold Ockenga, founder of the National Association of Evangelicals, proclaimed the entire welfare state the coming of the Antichrist, thus formally combining politics and apocalyptic in a way that had only been done informally hitherto. After the fall of the Soviet Union, once again various new predictions were made to explain why the old predictions failed; never once did evangelicalism reconsider its entire approach to church doctrine, and rejoin the consensus of the mainstream church in the hope of Christ's return. Rather, new data was found for yet new predictions of the end. Every international organization has figured into the prediction of the endtime, from the United Nations, to the European Common Market, to the European Union, to NATO, even including the World Council of Churches, all conglomerations of evil predicted in the Bible as signs of the final day now ready to appear. The terrible day of 9/11 immediately caused a scramble of new predictions about the entire Islamic world as the tool of Satan, and the imminent end of the world in a final battle in the Middle East. When that did not happen, a new enemy, and in due course a new savior, had to be found. Evangelical apocalyptic found Donald J. Trump.

Before we observe this astounding new turn, we need to pull back and see the big picture. Evangelical prediction of the endtime had from the beginning in the nineteenth century a strong element of innovation. It was *not* the traditional Christian view, as it liked to suggest, far from it; in fact, it was a new religious departure from the mainstream of orthodox Christian doctrine concerning the return of Christ based on Holy Scripture. The kinds of detailed predictions of daily world events were utterly new, and the ability to absorb each new era of unfolding history into an ever elongated version of the endtime was without parallel in Christianity based on the Bible. Secondly, it had become *highly* politicized. The coming of Christ was perhaps the final point, but there seemed to be less and less interest in that; it was all about the gore, the blood, the anarchy, the political turmoil leading up to that which drew people's attention. Indeed, there was very little left of *Christianity* in this supposedly Christian version of the end. It became largely a game of prediction, a kind of futurism attached most directly to a conservative political and cultural vision of good and evil. In short, it had become *secularized*. The secularized, evangelical, apocalypse, found its true fulfillment in Donald Trump. We now briefly sketch how and why that happened.

We begin with the why. Trump himself played directly into the apocalyptic drama of evangelicalism, whether by design or by happenstance. He did so in four ways. First, in traditional Christian eschatology, the focus is entirely upon *hope* in the coming kingdom of God through the return of Christ. There is struggle, even much suffering, but it is always accompanied by courage through the power and victory of the risen and exalted Lord: "In the world you face persecution. But take courage; I have conquered the world!," Jesus tells his disciples gathered in the upper room shortly before his crucifixion (John 16:33). Trump replaced that hope with *fear*; the cosmic struggle that now lay ahead, in the secularized apocalypse of evangelicalism, was a place of darkness, not light, of warning and danger, of dread and terror. Trump named every fear and made it palpable. Second, he turned the fears into a life-or-death struggle between *us* and *them*. Once again, traditional Christian eschatology recognized that all peoples, all nations, all humanity on earth, are already under the authority, grace, and blessing of the risen Christ. All authority in heaven and on earth has been given to me, the risen Christ tells his disciples, shortly before his ascension. Yet the secularized apocalypse of evangelicalism had long since twisted the biblical witness into a Manichean struggle of two entities, good and evil. Trump named those entities. America is good; all that is not America is evil. Third, in traditional eschatology, all who remain in the time between the times, in the time between the resurrection of Christ and his final return, are still sinners, even Christians. All are sinners; all need grace; all must daily turn from the old life, and live in the light of the new, which is Christ himself, the hope of glory. Trump appealed to the misguided secularized apocalypse of evangelicalism, and named a new opponent: it is not sin that you face, but *weakness*. I will not lead you to righteousness, for that is not your problem; I will lead you to *strength*, for that is what Christians need. And finally, in Christian eschatology there is a profound paradox of grace: as we are weak, so the power of Christ himself is made more perfect in our weakness. His power even now abides in us, so that precisely when we are at our weakest, we are strong through his strength. But what happens if Christ has been removed from the picture, as has happened in the secularized apocalypse of evangelicalism? What happens if this world is conceived as under the power of Satan, and ready to end at any moment? What is needed, if not a Strongman, to stem the tide of evil, and hold back the forces arrayed against the righteous? Donald Trump saw the need, and offered *himself*, as that very Strongman to the evangelical community. *I* will protect you; *I* will watch over your concerns; *I* will help you to be *powerful* again. Indeed, the very images of his campaign were a kind of secular apocalypse, whether explicitly orchestrated or not. He *descended* from on high, down the escalator in Trump Tower, to announce his candidacy, just as Christ "will descend from heaven" to gather his own on the final day (1 Thess 4:16); he spoke in his inaugural of the beginning of a *new millennium* that now dawns with his own presidency; he is surrounded, always, by *gold*, just as are the streets of the heavenly Jerusalem (Rev 21:21). The secular apocalypse of evangelicalism—now no longer attached to the person of Christ in any meaningful way, but rather an open-ended political and cultural vision of world battle between good and evil—was looking for a leader to fight by its side, and Donald Trump, alone of the GOP candidates in 2016, offered battle.

Without the slightest hesitation, evangelical voices spoke in unreserved affirmation of Trump. And it is essential to listen to the tenor of their full-throated endorsement of Trump, if true understanding is to be reached as to the *how* of evangelical embrace of his candidacy, and eventual presidency. The secularized apocalypse of evangelicalism lays out a vision of the endtime, with detailed predictions of how the world will unfold according to purported biblical prophecies. The astounding fact is that Donald Trump became *part* of the prophecy of the evangelical apocalypse. Trump was not only the Strongman supporting evangelicals; he had *himself* become part of the biblical vision of the endtime. To put it plainly: God himself elected Donald Trump president, and his election is already predicted in the Bible. That is the how; let us briefly trace some of the voices which embodied it in the evangelical community, where such ideas were, and are, widespread, if not universal.

Not long before her death, Phyllis Schlafly, a longtime leader in the religious conservative movement, spoke of Trump in the definitive words of finality that would become common: "He does look like he's the last hope . . .We don't hear anybody saying what he's saying. In fact, most of the people who ought to be lining up with him are attacking him."[4] Keep in mind that, at this point in the campaign, there were still several prominent evangelical candidates, people like Ted Cruz, Mike Huckabee, Jeb Bush. They were using religious language, but they didn't fit the mold of the secular evangelical apocalypse; only Trump

---

4. Strang, *God and Donald Trump*, 65.

did. There was one hope left, one last hope, and Trump was it. Pat Robertson chimed in once the nomination was secured for Trump: "If we don't win this election, you'll never see another Republican, and you'll have a whole different church structure."[5] Notice again the secular apocalypse, now *heavily* politicized; the fortunes of the GOP, and even the very fortunes of the church of Jesus Christ, are identical, and both rest in the hands of Donald Trump, whose election is *essential*. There is little doubt as to why Robertson feels this way, for he makes his point crystal clear: "I think this will be the last election that the Republicans have a chance of winning because you're going to have people flowing across the border, you're going to have illegal immigrants coming in, and they're going to be legalized, and they're going to be able to vote, and once that happens you can forget it."[6] The end times are here, and it is *fear* that moves evangelicals to act, more specifically fear of the *other*. Assuming that Robertson was not referring to illegal immigrants from Canada pouring over the border, it is quite clear that such a fear is more than tinged with racism; it is soaked in it. Michelle Bachmann is emphatic that 2016 is the final election, the last hour, the endtime of America: "If you look at the numbers of people who vote and who lives (sic) in the country and who Barack Obama and Hillary Clinton want to bring in to the country, this is the last election when we even have a chance to vote for somebody who will stand up for godly moral principles. This is it."[7] This is it; evangelicals were not looking for someone who understood the difference between sin and righteousness. They were looking for someone who understood the difference between strength and weakness, someone who knew the mechanisms of power, and how to wield them on behalf of evangelical interests. They were looking for a Strongman, *the* Strongman. Robert Jeffress outlines the Strongman motif with great clarity: "When I'm looking for a leader

---

5. Jones, *White Christian America*, 241.

6. Ibid., 242.

7. Ibid.

. . . I couldn't care less about that leader's temperament or his tone or his vocabulary. Frankly, I want the meanest, toughest, son of a gun I can find. And I think that's the feeling of a lot of evangelicals."[8] Apparently it was; and apparently it still is. But it has not always been so. Certainly the switch from a moral leader of character to a Strongman who knows how to conquer is a major sign of the slow but steady secularization of evangelical expectations of the endtime. Even attacks against Trump are attributed by Eric Metaxas to "demonic deception,"[9] as if the forces of light and darkness have now converged on this man and his mission to save Christian America. And finally, there were several evangelical Christian "prophets" who directly spoke of Trump as God's instrument to turn the tide of endtime disaster. Kim Clement announced that "Trump shall become a trumpet . . . I will raise up the Trump to become a trumpet," thus indicating that the biblical theme of the trumpet sound is none other than Donald Trump![10] Cindy Jacobs quoted Isaiah 59:19, "When the enemy shall come in like a flood, the Spirit of the Lord shall lift up a standard against him," and stated that God is indeed "preparing a patriot" to defend and lead the nation.[11] That patriot leader was Donald Trump. There were, and are, numerous others such prophecies of the coming of Trump. Perhaps the best known is that of Lance Wallnau, who noticed (before the election) that Cyrus the King is mentioned in Isaiah 45, and that the next president will be the forty-fifth president. Immediately he argued—and it became widely stated in the evangelical community—that Donald Trump is indeed the prophesied return of Cyrus the Persian King. In short, evangelical leaders had long spoken of the need for political figures to follow the teachings of the Bible. Here for the first time they reversed their position. It is not important for this president to follow the teaching of the

8. Fea, *Believe Me*, 39.
9. Brody and Lamb, *The Faith*, 305.
10. Strang, *God and Donald Trump*, 69.
11. Ibid.

Bible; rather, it is the Bible *itself* that *teaches* the coming of this president, Donald Trump.

Having observed the theological foundation for the evangelical embrace of Trump, we turn now to their vigorous support for several elements of Trumpism. We begin with the issue of *nationalism*, enshrined in the slogan "America First," first used of course by American sympathizers with the very Nazi-era policies we have discussed above. Trumpist nationalism can be briefly stated. A nation exists for one great purpose: to serve the self-interest of its own citizens. National self-interest is more than simply the highest moral good; it is immeasurable. It is that by which everything else *must be* measured. That which serves national self-interest is good; that which detracts from national self-interest is evil. There can be no half measures; in such a system, a total allegiance to nation, and to mutual loyalty within the nation, is essential. On the one hand, nationalism is the rule of the people, whose mutual pride will overturn any divisions. On the other hand, the will of the people is expressed in their elected leader, Donald Trump. It is expected that not only the Republican Party, but indeed the entire national body politic, will conform to, will coordinate with, the direction established by Trump, for his election is a mandate for all-embracing national conformity to a new direction, his direction. Thus, nationalism, populism, and authoritarianism, are merged into one.

And evangelicals support this new direction wholeheartedly. We listen again to some of their voices. In his sermon before the inauguration, Robert Jeffress spoke of how God himself had raised Trump (and Pence) up for a great, eternal purpose. He compares Trump to the Old Testament figure of Nehemiah, another powerful leader to restore the nation. As is well known to readers of the Bible, Nehemiah instituted the rebuilding of the walls around the broken city of Jerusalem, with its infrastructure in shambles. So, according to Jeffress, we understand: God is *not* against building walls! Jeffress then turns to praise Trump for how he has confounded his critics at every turn, just like Nehemiah confounded his critics. He concludes that Trump and his team have been called by God and elected by the people to do a great work. Jeffress expresses his certainty that Trump will be unstoppable in his endeavors. Why? No president in the history of the United States has had more natural gifts than Trump. Just as his campaign slogan was "Make America Great Again!," so the Bible promises the greatness of those nations whose God is the Lord. In summary, for Jeffress, Trump is nothing less than a figure like the great Nehemiah, appointed by God to raise up the nation of America after devastating loss during the Obama years to a new time of national greatness, starting with a campaign of building walls against all outsiders, especially to the south. Nationalism and white nativism coalesce in evangelical support for Trumpism. Jeffress offers American Christians encouragement, especially those who wonder if the best days are now behind us: "Has God removed His hands of blessing from us? But in the midst of that despair came November 8, 2016. It was on that day, November the 8th that God declared that the people, not the pollsters, were gonna choose the next president of the United States. And they chose Donald Trump."[12] For Jeffress, election day 2016 is nothing less than the biblical Day of the Lord. God and Trump; Trump and God. That is the new nationalism of the religious right.

We listen to the prayer of Paula White, delivered at the Republican National Convention in Cleveland, after Trump was nominated for President by the GOP. Throughout the prayer, the cadences of the new secular apocalypse of evangelicalism are present in the repeated formula: It is time . . . It is time . . . It is time . . . It is time . . . In the past there is darkness; now, with the future under the candidate Donald Trump, there is a "brighter future for America."[13] The wall between church and state collapses. America not only is to be understood in the light of the biblical sacred story, the national story of America *is* the divine sacred story on earth. America now has a holy calling in the world. America is now the "light that the world so desperately needs."[14] America now—in

---

12. Strang, *God and Donald Trump*, 169.

13. Brody and Lamb, *The Faith*, 219.

14. Ibid.

the age of Trump—upholds truth, and stands "for the way of our God."[15] America now raises up a standard against the forces of evil, again using the words of apocalyptic, in which it is presumed that America is now the good, and the rest of the world is now harboring the threat of evil. America seeks God's own anointing. God has parted the Red Seas for the nation, such that America itself is a miracle. America stands in God's own righteousness.

Lest we dismiss such sermons and prayers as mere piety, we must recognize that they reflect the nationalism of evangelical *theology*. In his treatise on *Politics According to the Bible*, Wayne Grudem argues that the goal of the church is to strive for "significant influence" on the state.[16] All citizens of the state must learn the type of government God reveals in the moral standards of the Bible; it is the duty of pastors to teach those moral standards to all citizens of the state, and to explain how they apply to every sphere of life. Citizens who vote *must know* the type of government God wants; and they can only learn that from the Bible. Without significant Christian influence, governments have no moral compass at all, and make mistakes on war, same-sex marriage, care for the environment, capital punishment, moral standards, and so forth. Only if Christians have major influence in society can a nation learn right from wrong. Having laid this foundation, Grudem then lays out the rudiments of his Christian nationalism. For example, taxes should be low; the best solution is a fixed rate of 10 percent for everyone. The Supreme Court should read the Constitution just like evangelicals read the Bible, according to the verbal sense alone (originialism), without consulting the history of its interpretation. Guns should be carried by everyone, though individual discretion is allowed. The National Education Association is against Christianity, and only school vouchers are biblical. If people over sixty-five can work, they should not be given Social Security. Climate change science is a hoax; more CO_2 is actually good for the environment. Torture and waterboarding are perfectly fine, and in

15. Ibid.
16. Grudem, *Politics*, 55.

some cases *not* using torture is a moral evil. There should be no homosexuals in the military, and no women in combat. Foreign aid is a mistake, a waste of money. And so forth, and so forth. Now, it seems rather obvious that Grudem is outlining what amounts to the party platform of the GOP, and calling it the biblical view. In fact, that is exactly what he concludes: "I have concluded in most of the preceding chapters that the policies endorsed by the leadership of the Republican Party have been much more consistent with biblical teaching."[17] According to Grudem, that even includes whether we should be given a choice of paper or plastic, a choice which is apparently a biblically mandated ordinance. Indeed, in the nationalistic theo-politics of Grudem, the two parties rest on two theologies, one right, the other wrong: "The differences between Democrats and Republicans today have great significance. These differences are not accidental, but stem from differing convictions about several moral and theological issues."[18] In his *Christian Ethics*, Grudem pursues the theme of nationalism even further. Nations include a sense of belonging that shapes a person's identity; a sense of pride in the nation, and the good things the nation has done, that only comes with a proper understanding of national history; a sense of security from attacks by violent evildoers whether from inside or outside the nation; a sense of obligation to defend the nation from unfair criticism; a sense of obligation to share the moral values and standards of the nation, which necessitates a common sense of the origin and history of the nation. Criticism of a nation, focus on ancient or minor mistakes of the nation, amount to opposition of the good of the nation, and will eventually destroy it.[19]

Now, we will in a moment turn to a theological critique of the nationalism expressed in these views, not only of Grudem, but of White and Jeffress, which are representative of many others. But one point here needs to be noted. The German Christians were

---

17. Ibid., 573.

18. Ibid., 590.

19. Grudem, *Christian Ethics*, 466–68.

obsessed with the need to coordinate the plans and aims of the church with the new formulation of the national good as defined in 1933. Here, the plans and aims of the church are simply folded into the party policies of the GOP, are identified with the national destiny of the United States, and are pledged in support of Donald Trump and his agenda. The language of the German Christians and the American evangelicals sound all too similar.

Before we continue our discussion of the *politics* of Trumpism, and evangelical support for it, we briefly now mention two issues of *policy*. The first concerns policy toward the state of Israel. Trump has begun the process of moving the US Embassy to Jerusalem; has approved the Israeli annexation of the Golan Heights; has given the green light to further settlements on the West Bank, all in radical change of direction from all previous US policy toward Israel, beginning in 1948. These moves make a two-state solution virtually impossible, leaving Israel with only one choice: becoming a permanent occupying state, with Palestinians a permanent underclass of non-citizens. Now, while it is widely known that Trump reads the Bible more, and knows the Bible better, than anyone else on earth, it seems somewhat likely that policy toward Israel in his administration is driven by Vice President Mike Pence, who is a well-known advocate of *Christian Zionism*. What does that mean? The phrase harks back to the idea of Jewish Zionism, and it is important to be precise. Zionism as it was originally formulated concerned a new state in Israel to harbor refugees from the growing force of anti-Semitism in Europe. It was a noble vision: a new, secular state where Jews would be welcome and secure. Over time, a *second* meaning emerged: Zionism as support for a Jewish state in which Palestinians have no part. Most people now use the word Zionist to describe the second of these ideas; but it is, I think, important, to realize that the original vision of Zionism was very different. Christians Zionists use the phrase *only* in the second sense; they certainly believe in a Jewish state in which Palestinians, and Arabs more generally, have no place at all. Moreover, they believe in the notion of a Greater Israel, that the borders of the modern state of Israel should be as they are as described in the Bible, which includes some territory belonging to Egypt, Jordan, and even Saudi Arabia. Once those new borders are established, and all Arabs are removed from Israel, Jerusalem once again becomes the capitol city of a Jewish state of Israel. The Dome of the Rock (Qubbat Al-Sakhrah)—built on the older Jewish Temple Mount, the third holiest site in Islam—will be razed to the ground. A new Jewish Temple will be built, and sacrifices will be resumed. It is at that point, in the evangelical view of the endtime, that Christ will return. Jews will either become Christians, or be destroyed. Such is the basic Christian Zionist view, and their reasons for supporting an expanded Israel without Palestinians present at all.

Since the era of Menachim Begin, the prime minister of Israel from 1977 to 1983, it has been common for Israeli leaders to endorse Christian Zionism in America, for obvious political reasons. Clearly, as the religious right grew in power in the United States, so too did a radical shift in American foreign policy toward Israel become inevitable. But it is important to recognize exactly what is at stake; for Trump himself has brought that out most clearly. Christian Zionism has no interest in the fate of the Jewish people as a people; its interest is in the endtime prophecies of the Bible. That is not to doubt their sincerity, not at all. Rather, it is simply to recognize what is sincerely and openly stated by Christian Zionists: the endtime will come when Christ returns to the rebuilt Temple, and Jews either convert or perish. We will offer in the next chapter a very different understanding of the biblical witness to God's enduring covenant with the Jewish people, as outlined in Romans 9–11 and embraced now by mainstream Christian doctrine based on Holy Scripture; but we here can only state the rather clear point that such a view as embraced by Christian Zionism is inherently anti-Semitic. Jews—Israel—are merely a tool for Christian Zionist calculations of the endtime; they are but human pieces of a cosmic struggle, in which only the Christian evangelicals are on the side of good. At any rate, there is little doubt that Christian Zionism—which is supported by a vast majority of evangelicals in America—is decidedly in favor of Trumpism. Once again, he is not only considered a supporter of the apocalyptic movement of endtime prophecy, but an actual figure *within* it. The foremost Christian Zionist of our time is John Hagee. According to Hagee, Trump is the one last wall standing against the final collapse. If Trump fails to accomplish his goals, according to Hagee, there will be a "liberal dictatorship."[20] Such a dictatorship will bring a New World Order, which is shorthand for the advent of the great Tribulation. People will be forced to speak one language, use one currency, have one religion, all under the United Nations and the ACLU. Donald J. Trump is, alone, all that stands in the way. If he fails, from that moment on, the endtime unfolds toward Armageddon. Robert Jeffress, another strong Christian Zionist, and profound Trump supporter, was present at the dedication of what will become the new embassy in Jerusalem, and offered an official prayer. As he prayed, he spoke of the Messiah, the fulfillment of prophecies, the great leadership of President Donald J. Trump given by God, a leader who stands on the right side of God. One thing he did not pray for? The Jewish people.

We consider very briefly as well the policy of Trump concerning climate change, its impact upon the world, and the proper response to it for the sake of future generations as well as the health of the planet. It is well known that Donald Trump is the greatest scientist who ever lived, smarter than all other scientists. Indeed, his IQ is one of the highest ever. So it is not surprising that Trump has himself determined the scientific accuracy of climatology and related sciences. Despite the established consensus among global scientists that human impact upon the environment through the use of fossil fuels is a direct cause of global warming, Donald Trump has determined that the entire notion is false. More than that, it is a widespread scientific hoax, a con job. More than that, it is an expensive hoax, a total con job based on faulty science, a canard, fictional, mythical, and frankly truly stupid. We have yet to see the data upon which he bases this remarkable set of scientific observations, but doubtless this will be forthcoming in the appropriate journals. In accordance with his scientific conclusions,

---

20. Hagee, *Empire*, 215.

Trump pulled the United States out of the Paris Climate Accord, a landmark in the modern movement toward a sustainable world. Along with his scientific expertise, he added another rationale: American sovereignty. Nationalism and science ultimately must coordinate; science is politics, politics is science. It is clear that the United States entered the accord freely, under no coercion; thus, it seems quite clear that Trump means American sovereignty over its *own natural resources*. America has a right to do with earth what it pleases, at least that portion of earth within its borders. There is no need to ask concerning the *consequences* of American actions, for the notion of national sovereignty is self-evident and self-authenticating in Trumpism. America First applies to the earth as well. With these views in mind, we ask: what is the evangelical response to the total dismissal of modern science by Trumpism, especially as it relates to climate change?

Of course, evangelicalism has its own long history of dismissing modern science. It early rejected Darwin, as a threat to the biblical witness to the divine creation of the cosmos, and since that rejection has had a running battle with virtually every element of modern scientific discovery. So it is not altogether surprising to learn that evangelical theology follows Trumpism in rejecting climate science altogether; and moreover, arguing for an even *more* robust human exploitation of the natural world. Consider the argument of Wayne Grudem. God has given human beings not only the right, but the *responsibility*, to exploit and use to the fullest the resources of the creation: "This responsibility to 'subdue' the earth and 'have dominion' over it implies that God expected Adam and Eve and their descendants to explore and develop the earth's resources . . ."[21] It is not clear how Grudem has become aware of God's "implication," but he is certain that the Bible commands unlimited use of earth by humanity. He outright condemns environmentalism as a sin against God; God never meant the earth to be left untouched by human exploitation. In fact, environmentalism is itself the greatest threat to the health of the planet. Rather, the

21. Grudem, *Christian Ethics*, 1101.

unlimited development of the earth's natural resources is a self-validating moral good. If God put sources of energy in the earth, such as coal, does it not stand to reason that he not only wants but *expects* us to use them? Indeed, the more energy we use—in travel, in labor, in household appliances, in climate control, and so forth—the more enriching our lives become. Grudem concludes: "Using all available energy sources is a wonderful ability that God has provided the human race, and it marks us as far above the animal kingdom, as creatures truly made in the image of God."[22] Being able to exploit the earth for its unlimited natural resources marks the image of God in humankind, and makes humanity far superior to all animals. God put wood, coal, oil, and natural gas on the earth for us to use it. It is morally wrong to feel guilty about using these resources, and global warming science is morally wrong because it makes people feel guilty: "Rather than allowing us to use God's good gifts with thanksgiving, they load us with guilt for doing so. Therefore, they rob people of the motivation to thank God for the wonderful things he has given."[23] In short, Grudem has thought the problem through, as he states, and has concluded that the only possible reason God put coal, oil, and natural gas in the earth, is "so that we could have abundant, easily transportable sources of fuel for use in various applications."[24] That being the case, science is wrong. It should also be added that Grudem is convinced that the science of global warming is really about government intervention in human life: "The controversy over global warming is to a very large degree a controversy over human liberty versus government control."[25] Because government control is wrong, therefore the science must be invalid. Science is politics; politics is science.

---

22. Ibid., 1133.

23. Ibid., 1144.

24. Ibid., 1143. It is a curious argument. God also put water hemlock (*cicuta douglasii*) and the deadly mushroom *amanita phalloides* on the earth. Are we to enjoy them as well, because they are there, and suffer the consequences? "The wise are cautious and turn away from evil, but the fool throws off restraint and is careless" (Prov 14:16).

25. Ibid., 1161.

We return now to the broader analysis of the politics of Trumpism, and evangelical support for it, concluding with two final issues. Trumpism is a political boundary language. That is to say, it defines its inner core—nationalism—by excluding the other. It does so in two ways, the first of which is both overt, and external. I am referring to Trump's absolute opposition to immigrants and immigration. To be a follower of Trumpism is to be a complete opponent of immigration as a threat to the health and well-being of national life. Trump wasted no time in making this quite clear. After descending from on high, surrounding by glittering gold, Trump announced his policy, not only of no tolerance for illegal immigrants, but of active discouragement of all immigration, especially from the South and from Muslim countries. His words were not shaded in the language of policy, but of fear and hate: "The US has become a dumping ground for everybody else's problems . . . When Mexico sends its people, they're not sending their best. They're not sending you. They're not sending you. They're sending people that have lots of problems, and they're bringing those problems with us. They're bringing drugs. They're bringing crime. They're rapists . . ."[26] In fact, of course, Trump is describing a reality that does not exist. Since 2014, most immigrants from the South have been *families*, and they have come seeking asylum, not seeking to enter the United States illegally. Nevertheless, the message remains clear: you are not welcome here! We are full! In order to make that message fully clear, the Trump administration separated children from their families. It is still not known exactly how many were separated, but the number was certainly in the thousands; the exact number may never be known, so shoddy was the record-keeping. Most have been reunited, but not all; it is in fact entirely possible that some children will *never* be reunited with their families; and the United States of America is responsible for breaking up these families, turning even young children into orphans. These are not drug dealers; these are not rapists; these are *children*, some mere *infants*. Some will likely never see their

---

26. Brody and Lamb, *Faith*, 142–43.

parents again because of the actions of the Trump administration, and even those who do will be scarred for life. The policy has, for now, ceased; but the message has not: you are not welcome here! We are full!

Evangelicalism is a *religious* boundary language, though the boundary has shifted over time. Until the fall of the Soviet Union, communism was seen as the great Enemy. After the events of 9/11, it was suddenly Muslims, and Islam in general. It was not limited, not by any means, to the perpetrators of the dastardly deeds of that day, or their supporters; it was a war of one religious civilization (Christendom) against another religious civilization (the Islamic world). Franklin Graham pontificated concerning the entire Muslim world: it is a "wicked and evil religion."[27] Pat Robertson carefully and objectively described the Koran as "teaching warfare so at the core of this faith is militant warfare,"[28] apparently forgetting momentarily that there are wars in the Bible. Indeed, Robertson called Muslims "worse than the Nazis."[29] Jerry Falwell called the Prophet Muhammed "a terrorist,"[30] while C. Peter Wagner called Allah—the Arabic word for God—a "high ranking demon."[31] Again, evangelicalism had always defined itself over against an enemy, indeed an Enemy, which is the absolute embodiment of all Evil in the world. That cosmic dualism is, as we have seen, a part of the apocalyptic framework which sets it apart from mainstream Christian doctrine; indeed, mainstream Christianity itself is one with the enemy.

A new enemy was added—an adjunct, as it were—in the mid 2000s: and that is immigrants. It is not that evangelical opposition to immigrants predates Trumpism, so much as that both grew from the same fertile soil: which is the Tea Party. Reacting against the presidency of Barack Obama, and in particular the Affordable

27. Fitzgerald, *Evangelicals*, 475.
28. Ibid.
29. Ibid.
30. Ibid.
31. Ibid.

Care Act, the Tea Party—which virtually overlapped with white evangelicalism—revolted at the notion that help was being extended to the young, the poor, and especially to immigrants, help that should rightly be returned to the true American citizens from which it had been stolen. No more handouts! And above all, immigrants were to blame for the new, creeping socialism. Gary Bauer put it this way: "Hyphenated Americans put other countries and affiliations first, and they drive a wedge into the heart of 'one nation.'"[32] Immigrants shatter the unity of the nation; and the unity of the nation and the unity of religion are one and the same. One country, one God, one people! Tony Perkins points out: "do we have an immigration policy that is serving to strengthen the cultural fabric of the nation, which has a great influence on the family? The answer is no."[33] Notice the shape of the argument. The goal is the "value of the family." The means to the goal, according to Perkins, is his version of American culture, which is of course "Christian culture." Therefore, on the basis of "family values" immigrants must be excluded. The irony of course should at least be pointed out that many immigrants from the South are Christian, have deeply held family ties, and have contributed enormously to American culture. It should also at least be mentioned that in the Germany of 1930 anti-Semitism was a well-worn traditional family value.

We will briefly rehearse the arguments against immigration now familiar in evangelical circles. But before we do, one fact needs to be pointed out, lest it be lost in the chaos of the moment. Evangelicals were *not* anti-immigrant until very recently. There were of course exceptions, as there always are. Charles Hodge, the great Princeton architect of modern conservative evangelical theology, was convinced that immigrants were bringing Roman Catholicism to America, and would turn it into a papal state. More recently, Francis Schaeffer blamed immigrants for the rise of secularity, which he taught a generation of evangelicals to fear as the

---

32. Fitzgerald, *Evangelicals*, 605.

33. Ibid.

great Enemy. But these are not the norm. The fact is, evangelicals were, until very recently, open to immigrants, and welcomed them into their churches and into their homes. Moreover, they made no distinction between so-called legal and illegal immigrants. There is absolutely no sign of this distinction in the literature of evangelical discussion of immigration until very recently. Immigrants are immigrants, however they got here; that is, until the mid-2000s. It was at that point—during the presidency of Obama, with the rise of the Tea Party—that white evangelicals suddenly began to highlight immigration as a *negative* issue rather than a *positive* opportunity, and seized upon the distinction between legal and illegal immigrants as a way to force through an anti-immigrant political position. They turned to the Bible for support, even though the Bible makes no distinction between legal and illegal immigrants; only modern nation-states make such a distinction. Reading such a distinction into the Bible is simply a way of forcing the Bible to agree with the party platform of the Tea Party, and ultimately the GOP, and ultimately Donald Trump. Indeed, as we will see later, the Bible has a *great deal* to say about immigrants; and what it says is quite clear, and quite profound.

With these points of background in mind, we now outline the current evangelical position on immigration, which is in fact scarcely distinguishable from Trumpism. The leading evangelical theologian Wayne Grudem makes a sustained argument. According to Grudem—and evangelicalism generally—the realm of government generally, including government policy concerning immigration, falls under the category of *common grace*. Common grace is to be carefully distinguished from the grace of God in Jesus Christ; common grace does not flow from the cross and resurrection of Christ. It is not part of salvation, not redemptive. The idea of common grace actually stems from the nineteenth-century conservative neo-Calvinist Abraham Kuyper, and is part of the innovative complex of ideas that sets conservative evangelicalism apart from traditional, mainstream Christianity. The notion of common grace explains, for example, why certain parts of the Bible, such as the Sermon on the Mount, are said not to apply to the issues of immigration; they only apply to "saving grace," which comes through Christ. Similarly, Grudem systematically avoids using the phrase "social justice" in his ethics. He argues that it leads to a "victim mentality" in society, and the phrase is not in the Bible, so it should be avoided (curiously, neither is the phrase "common grace").[34] The grace of God involved in immigration does not come through Christ, and it is not a matter of social justice; with these provisos in mind, he lays out his case. First, Grudem follows a strictly nationalist argument. Immigration should benefit the United States; and all questions regarding immigration policy should revolve around the question of what benefit redounds to the priorities of the nation. Immigration must not be based, that is, on the condition of *need* among the immigrants, such as political oppression. It must be based on the *desire* of the nation to allow them in. Indeed, according to Grudem, an immigration hearing should not circle around the validity of appeals for asylum, but rather evidence of possible positive contributions to the national self-interest: "advancing the well-being of the nation."[35] Secondly, the fact that immigrants are not "assimilating" into the larger American culture—he nowhere defines exactly what this means—but instead cluster in "ethnic communities" is a major drawback to immigration. "These people," he states (with no evidence) "drain more resources from the nation than they provide."[36] Third, Grudem argues for a permanent wall to be built along the entire "1,951 mile long border" between the United States and Mexico.[37] He offers a variety of tips on how the wall should be built, such as a double wall, with high-tech monitoring devices, and so forth, apparently sharing a common expertise in wall technology with Donald Trump. Fourth, every immigrant must be taught to speak English fluently, not only because English is our national language, but because—as Grudem's own

34. Grudem, *Christian Ethics*, 961–62.
35. Grudem, *Politics*, 472.
36. Ibid.
37. Ibid., 474.

international travels have confirmed—English is a valuable tool for world travel. Why not learn English and see the world? If immigrants are to come here, they must be part of the nation; for we are "one nation and one society."[38] And finally, what of the obligation of the church to illegal immigrants? Churches can in some cases help them find good lawyers, but in all cases they must tell them to leave the country. "Illegal immigrants are obligated before God to obey the immigration laws of the United States";[39] with that statement, the responsibility of the church ends in respect to illegal immigrants. With this outline of contemporary evangelical views of immigration in mind, it is not difficult to understand how readily this religious community embraced what Donald Trump had to offer; they were looking into a mirror.

As a political boundary language, Trumpism defines an overt, external other, to be attacked and resisted at all costs, namely immigrants. The country is full! Keep them out! It also, however, defines an *internal*, and *covert* other, an all the more insidious reference because the language used is coded rather than openly expressed. And that other is defined in racial terms; Trumpism is the normalization of white America, and the cultural and social exclusion of people of color. The nostalgic appeal of Trump to a time in the past when America was still great—and the desire to make it great again—is an appeal to a past in which black people were segregated, were denied the right to vote, were treated as second-class citizens at every level of society; and before that were lynched, and were enslaved. The saying "Make America Great Again," for people who are not white, sounds the same thing as declaring "Make America White Again." America has of course even now not outgrown its racism, not at all; but the very *basis* of Trump's presidency was and is to turn the clock backward to a time in which even the gains already made along the lines of civil rights for all Americans are erased. Greatness means whiteness. Trump's repeated failures as president to condemn the acts of white nationalism, including the

38. Ibid., 477.
39. Ibid., 481.

most notorious case in Charlottesville (during which he declared that both sides, the white supremacists and their opponents, have equivalent validity), simply flows from the very basis of his candidacy and presidency. How can he condemn that which he espouses so deeply that he built it into his very slogan? When Trump speaks to Christians, he is speaking to white American Christians, and he speaks as their great Protector: "America is better when people put their faith into action. As long as I am your president, no one is ever going to stop you from practicing your faith or from preaching what's in your heart. We will always stand up for the right of all Americans to pray to God and to follow his teachings."[40] It is of course the First Amendment of the Constitution of the United States that guarantees freedom of religion, not the power of the president. But white American evangelicalism has increasingly seen itself as an embattled ethno-religious heritage, about to lose its privileged status within society. These words of Donald Trump quoted above are words of the endtime; I am your last chance to keep your status! Keep me in office, and you keep yourself in control of American culture; lose my presidency, and you lose your place in society! It is that bargain—ultimately racial in both tone and content—that white evangelicals reached out and accepted.

First some background. In the 1960s, Martin Luther King, Jr. reminded the church and the nation of the biblical-prophetic truth that all are created equal; that we cannot judge a person by the color of their skin, but rather by the content of their character. On the basis of the civil rights movement that he (and others) advanced, the great civil rights legislation of the decade arose: the Civil Rights Act of 1957 establishing the Civil Rights Commission, the Civil Rights Act of 1960 establishing federal inspection of local voter registration polls to eliminate illegal literacy tests and poll taxes; the Civil Rights Act of 1964, prohibiting discrimination based on race, color, religion, sex, and national origin; and the Civil Rights Act of 1968 prohibiting discrimination in the sale, rental, and financing of housing based on race, creed, and national

40. Brody and Lamb, *Faith*, 303.

origin. All of these acts were specifically designed to tear down the walls of racial prejudice and discrimination. And all would require federal government protection in order to be enforced.

Now, while some evangelicals were opposed to the entire civil rights movement, others did not reject the civil rights movement outright. Many saw the movement as a threat to their way of life; others saw it as simply irrelevant to their faith. Those who did accept it usually framed the issue in terms of personal attitude: we can change how we *see* other races, without changing the social *structures* of racism. In the end, evangelicals did not, by and large, *directly* and *openly* reject the claims of blacks for full equal rights. But that is not the same thing as saying that they fully accepted the movement, and the vast social and cultural shift it precipitated. While they may have accepted the *claims* of civil rights, they at the same time rejected the *mechanisms* by which those rights could be established and secured. They did not say: we oppose civil rights! They said, instead, we oppose big government! For the simple fact is that opposition to "big government" would accomplish the same end. If there were no enforcement by the federal government of civil rights legislation, there would be no change. And that is of course what mattered; it was *change* that evangelicals opposed. Their opposition to big government was a racial protest, a racist protest. But it was *covert*, not overt. And it was also a door through which other social and cultural issues would soon enter, during the subsequent decades: opposition to women's equal rights, opposition to the equal rights of homosexuals and lesbians, opposition to same-sex marriage, and so forth. In each case, the same mantra could be chanted: big government, big government! Behind it all, however, was one simple fact: by opposing the role of the federal government *directly*, evangelicals were opposing the enforcement of civil rights for all *indirectly*.

With the election of the first African American as president of the United States in 2008, the issue of government, and the issue of race, could no longer be dealt with indirectly; they were now *identical*. What had been covert, now necessarily became overt. Just days after the election of Obama, Pat Robertson's Christian

Coalition put out an email to all the subscribers: "We will soon be celebrating the 400th anniversary of the first Thanksgiving and God has still not withheld his blessings upon this nation, although we now richly deserve such condemnation. We have a lot to give thanks for, but we also need to pray to our Heavenly Father and ask Him to protect us from those enemies, outside and within, who want to see America destroyed."[41] Why does America suddenly, just days after electing its first black president, deserve divine condemnation? And who are the enemies within, apparently so obvious to Robertson and his followers? He makes things much more clear by attaching a picture, a family gathered around a table giving thanks. They are all white. Over the table is the caption: "defending America's Godly Heritage." We have already recorded above the incessant evangelical attacks on Obama: on his faith (he is a Muslim!), his birthplace (he is not an American!), his character (he is a schemer!). The attacks on Obama were soon followed by several more overt attacks on black people in general. Here is how Franklin Graham addresses the protestors in Ferguson and the Black Lives Matter movement generally: "Listen up—Blacks, Whites, Latinos, and everybody else. Most police shootings can be avoided. It comes down to respect for authority and obedience. If a police officer tells you to stop, you stop. If a police officer tells you to put your hands in the air, you put your hands in the air. If a police officer tells you to lay down face first with your hands behind your back, you lay down face first with your hands behind your back. It's as simple as that. Even if you think the police officer is wrong—YOU OBEY."[42] Consider the tone: Listen up! Obey! Authority! Obedience! He sounds for all the world like a plantation owner addressing his slaves. Be that as it may, think for a moment back to the civil rights movement. Think of the marchers crossing the Edmund Pettus Bridge in Selma, Alabama. They marched peacefully, nonviolently. But they marched *disobediently*. They were *disobeying* unjust laws, and were willing to pay the consequences, even unlawful physical

41. Jones, *White Christian America*, 83.
42. Ibid., 148.

attack by lawful authority. Had the civil rights movement followed the barked commands of Franklin Graham (or of Bull Connor), there would be no civil rights legislation. Thankfully, they followed the wise counsel of Martin Luther King instead: always be peaceful, always be nonviolent, but do not be afraid to disobey unjust laws, for that is your moral responsibility. An unjust law is no law at all, King rightly declared.

The America that Donald Trump wants to make great again is an America *before* civil rights were fully recognized and established for all people. Evangelicalism has sadly bought into his contorted vision, because it is has carried it in its own nightmares for some time. David Brody and Scott Lamb, authors of a "spiritual biography" widely touted by evangelical followers of Trump, put it this way: "It's no secret that white, evangelical Christians, while still dominant politically, see their culture slipping away. They're not the majority they once were and they've been looking for that fierce protector. And along came Donald Trump . . ."[43] To speak of white evangelical Christianity is to speak of an ethno-religious heritage; it is *not* to speak of the church of Jesus Christ. But no matter; they continue, dreaming nostalgically of the "cultural link . . . with the past: a connection that encompassed patriotism, respect for God and Country, a disdain for political correctness, and a restoration of good old-fashioned Judeo-Christian values."[44] Good old-fashioned Judeo-Christian values; that is, a world where white people are at the top of the social scale, and people of color are at the bottom. Disdain for political correctness; a world where white supremacists are given equal cultural space with supporters of civil rights. Respect for God and country; a world where laws are obeyed, even when unjust, and civil disobedience is forbidden. Brody and Lamb are certainly correct in this: it was a dream which "struck political gold for Trump and for evangelicals."[45] White evangelicals gained the power they sought and were afraid of

43. Brody and Lamb, *Faith*, 316.

44. Ibid., 317.

45. Ibid.

losing. Yet at what price? Their message to the world is now: "Make America Great Again!"

Where is Christ? And where is the cross, upon which he died for the sins of the world?

4

The Gospel of Jesus Christ

How are we, the community of faith in Jesus Christ, to respond to the challenge of Trumpism, and the support of American evangelicalism for it? We begin by remembering.

We remember first of all that we are hardly the first generation of the church, or for that matter of the larger human community, to pass through hard times. Even in these pages we have briefly charted the course of Hitler and Nazism, and the high price paid by those who were faithful to the gospel in the face of German Christian support for the Third Reich. From the very beginning of the church to the present day our mothers and fathers in the faith have faced challenges equal to, and far greater, than we face. They have persevered with eager joy and constant hope despite the struggles they faced, often even unto death; how can we draw back now?

We remember second of all the promise of Christ by which we live, and by which the church is sustained: "I will be with you always." The promise was not given and then washed away by time; the living promise is the *event* of Christ's own direct and immediate presence in the life of the church in each new generation. We now face challenges in many ways very different from the past; and yet, Jesus Christ is the same, yesterday, today, and always. We will not chase after falsehood, but expose it. We will not run after political and religious error and distortion, but seek to correct it. We will not be fooled by the false promises of authoritarian politics, but will resist them, and if it be so, defeat them. Not because *we* are able, but because *he* is able, far more able than we can think or imagine.

We remember finally the goal of our lives. We do not in the end care about the judgment of the world. We can sit very loose on the opinions of others, especially the powerful and the influential. For in the end we are responsible to One who is coming to judge the whole world in truth and in righteousness. We live for him, we wait for him, we long for him. Our love for him casts out every fear. And so remembering we begin our question: what is the gospel of Jesus Christ, and what does it say about Trumpism?

With the church of all times and places, we turn for our answer to the Scriptures. Holy Scripture is the one norm of faith and practice in the church. The Scriptures are not a dead letter from the past; they are theologically shaped to address every new generation of the community of faith. The Scriptures are God's own word to the church and the world. We mean that first of all quite literally, that is, in the literal sense. The very human words of the Bible are, by the miracle of the Holy Spirit, the Word of God. But we cannot stop there, as evangelicalism does; we cannot hunt here and there for proof-texts to make our point. The Scriptures are shaped theologically to bear witness to one subject matter: which is Jesus Christ. The rule of Christ alone is the truth by which the Scriptures are rightly understood, and rightly measured. There is in the Bible a pattern of truth, a content, a rule of faith and life, to be carefully observed and faithfully rendered. We find the truth of the Bible only by following the words to their true subject-matter, which is Christ the Lord; but by the same token, we understand the words of Scripture truly only in the light of Christ, and only in his light do we see light.

Let us make our point crystal clear. There are two ways of reading the Bible. On the one hand, we can follow the *logic of confirmation*. We can pick up the Bible, knowing beforehand what we wish to find or prove, and aha! we find and prove it with just the right verses. We want to prove that a wall must be built on the southern border. So we consult our concordance under "wall" and find a passage where a wall is built. There it is! Nehemiah built a wall! Therefore, Trump is right to build a wall! Trump is Nehemiah! That is the logic of confirmation. It is a matter of *using* the Bible to confirm a political position we have already arrived at, whether it accords with the pattern of truth found in the Bible or not. It is a matter of turning to the Bible to confirm what we already know, or think we know, about God and his will. The logic of confirmation is the tried and true method of false doctrine in church history.

The other approach, which is the way of the mainstream church from the beginning, is the *logic of discovery*. We come to the Scriptures blind, seeking sight. We come to the Scriptures wounded, seeking healing. We come confused, disturbed, uncertain; and we seek direction, illumination, wisdom. Now, we cannot jump over our own shadow. We all bring our own time, our own resources, even our own personalities, to the study of the Scriptures. But when we come in prayer, in worship, and in care for the weak and vulnerable; when we come seeking to know what we do not understand, the miracle of God's Spirit guides us to fresh understanding and fresh growth. We discover new truths we have never seen; we recognize new insights, which we have never even fully considered. Indeed, we encounter nothing less than the *new world* of God in the Bible, which turns the world in which we live upside down. The first are last; the weak are strong; the mighty are cast down; for God is *God*. The new world of the Bible is not an alternative universe, not an imaginary world; we suddenly realize that is the very world in which we live and move and have our being. God is *God* even right here and right now, in the midst of the struggles we face.

And when the biblical witness provides us with a range of texts often in tension with one another, we are given by Christ himself a rule of faith by which to decide the best interpretation: and that is the rule of twofold love of God and neighbor. That interpretation is right which leads to love of God above all things, and love of neighbor as oneself; all others are to be cast aside and forgotten.

The gospel is the *event* of God's freely given mercy and grace through the cross and resurrection of Jesus Christ. On the cross, Jesus Christ took the sins of the world upon himself, and bore them away. He died the death of the one great Sinner, and in so doing put sin itself to death. In the resurrection of Christ, the miracle of God's free gift of love brings into being a new world, a new age, a new humanity. The risen Christ even now is Lord over all reality; even now his authority over all creation knows no limits.

Who was there at his death, at the cross? Were you there? asks the beautiful African American spiritual. And the answer of course is yes; we were all there, all humanity. The Romans were there, pitiless and brutal. The state was there, venal and corrupt. God's people were there, crying out for his death. The disciples were there, hiding in shame and fear. Peter was there, ready to deny him three times. The soldiers were there, beating him, torturing him, hanging him on the cross. All humanity was there. The cross draws a line. It is *not* and *never will be* a line between "them" and "us." That is an ethnic-religious nationalism that the cross itself utterly *condemns* as foreign to the gospel of Jesus Christ. There is no them, there is no us. There is, on the one side of the line, the one Righteous, Jesus Christ himself; and on other side the whole of humanity, you and me, all of us, in every nation and culture, in all times and places. And on the cross Jesus says, to us all: Father forgive them. That is the gospel: the free forgiveness of sins through the cross of Jesus Christ that comes to all. We were lost, and now are found; we were blind, but now we see. The gift does not come to some; it comes to all, to the whole of humanity, for whom Christ died. He holds the whole world in his hands.

The resurrection of Christ brings newness of life. The risen Christ even now surrounds the whole world, the whole cosmos, with the glory of his love. There is no corner of this earth, this creation, where the love of the risen Christ is not present. He gathers into his great banquet of love, not those who are distracted by their dealings with the world, but those who live day to day, those who can scarcely get by, those who live outside the economic security of society. And they come. He reaches beyond the centers of power and influence to the nations, to the coastlands, to the farthest reaches of humanity beyond every border and every boundary. And they come. He does not accept those who are proud of their achievement; who stand on the glory of their own great civilization and merit; he gathers into his arms those who are burdened, those who are bowed down by heavy labor, those who are overwhelmed by life's mistakes, those who have reached the very end of their resources. And they come. His merciful love gathers in those who mourn, those who make peace where there is no peace, those who live with humility, those who are despised and neglected. The sinner in his sight is welcomed; the self-righteous and self-affirming walks away empty. Whether people come early or later into his embrace, they are always welcome; all laborers in his vineyard receive the same wages, north and south, east and west, for all are his servants, to be judged by no one. His ingathering love breaks down every wall, crosses every border, overcomes every barrier, erases every boundary, until the whole world finds itself in his loving arms. Christ has died; Christ is risen; Christ will come again. That is the gospel.

The risen Christ gathers unto himself a people, a community of faith, the church. The role of the church is not to be *separate* from humanity; the role of the church is to be a *sign* in the midst of humanity of God's ultimate will for the whole of humankind. Here in the church there are offices; but there is no status, or rank, or privilege. The church is gathered into a unity, but it is not built on the principle of sameness, but diversity. Only the genuine diversity of the church and its gifts builds true unity. The church is universal throughout the earth; there are churches in every nation, but there are no nationalist churches. There is only one church among all nations and peoples of the earth. The church lives for Christ; he alone is Head of the church. Through time the church has learned, time and again, to resist unlawful and overbearing authority. It has leaned toward, and finally leaned into, democracy; because Christ alone is Head of the church, there can be no earthly king, no earthly prince or ruler. Power in the state is to be shared, spread around, grounded; it is not to flow from the top down because the true Head of the church and Ruler of all creation has already turned the way of the world upside down.

The church is not the state; the state is not the church. The separation of church and state is for the sake of the *church* as much as it is for the sake of the state. Yet, Jesus Christ, we confess, is Ruler of both church and state. They are not two separate realms; there is not one grace of God that rules the state (so-called common grace) and another grace of God that rules the church (the grace of Christ). Common grace is a pagan idea. The Bible knows only one grace: and that is God's free grace in the gospel, which is Jesus Christ crucified and risen. So, if church and state are not the same, yet are not separate but both under Christ, how are they related? It is best to think of them by *analogy*. Lessons we have learned in the church, in the community of faith, do not apply *directly* to the state; nevertheless, there are *analogies* that can be useful and instructive.

For example, the Spirit gives gifts to the church, gathering into one the people of God; yet it is the ordinary gifts of ordinary Christians that are upheld by Scripture as the vital element enlivening the mission and message of the community of faith. Even so, by analogy, in the realm of the state, it is the ordinary citizen who provides the true strength of democratic society, which gathers purpose and direction from the bottom up, not from the top down. Or again, in the church we learn to avoid idolatry, the worship of anything that is not God. By analogy, in the state there is the firm realization that unchecked power in and for itself is a destructive force, a threat to the well-being—even at times the very existence—of the common good.

With all these things in mind, we now turn to the question: how should mainstream Christianity respond to the politics of Trumpism, and evangelical support for Trump, in the light of the gospel? We will follow the main points outlined in the previous chapter, in turn. And we will turn to the pages of Scripture for instruction.

We begin with the figure of Trump, and the politics of Trumpism. Trump himself is a brutalist. As his tens of thousands of tweets make abundantly clear, he not only espouses the moral right of the strong over the weak, he bullies the weak, destroys them, and having destroyed them buries them forever. His words are the weapons of mass destruction. Evangelicals tell us that this is all fine and normal, that a strong leader is needed in such a time as ours. We need a mean son of a gun! Let us turn to the Scriptures and ask: is such brutality in conformity to the living will of God?

Often the Bible gives its most profound moral instruction, not in didactic argument, but in narratives, in stories. Consider the story of Nabal (1 Sam 25). David has already been anointed the new king by Samuel, but he and his small band of soldiers are on the run from King Saul in the wilderness. David is at his breaking point; he and his men need help. So they turn to Nabal, a man of inherited wealth. We quickly learn Nabal's character: he is a short-tempered, stubborn bully, who has no ability to think beyond the surface appearance of things. He has wealth in land and sheep, and is accustomed to throwing his weight around, always mean-spirited and thoughtless. The only credit that goes to this boorish man is that he has a kind, wise, and generous wife, Abigail. When David asks Nabal for help, this surly and foolish man simply reacts: he attacks David! David is a runaway slave! I will give him nothing! It is the classic tactic of the counterpuncher, with no interest in the truth, who sees in every situation a petty struggle for power and supremacy. Nabal is so *sure* he sees in David's request for help the real situation; in fact he sees nothing at all, a man without a genuine clue about real human life. He has no *empathy*, no ability to understand life from the point of view of another person, especially another person in need. The Hebrew text has a little fun at his expense; Nabal in Hebrew simply means: The Fool. Only Abigail truly understands, and renders aid to David and his men.

The way of the fool, the way of the brutalist, the way of the mean-spirited, is the way of toxic individualism. I alone can do it! I will defeat all enemies! If punched, I will punch back a hundred times harder! Here there is no possibility for empathy, no possibility for genuine humanity; for genuine humanity is defined by our mutual obligations to one another in civil society, especially obligations revealed to us in times of need. The way of the brutalist has already been defeated by the cross of Jesus Christ, who endured every abuse against himself from sinful humanity. Words that wound and demean and hurt—words that despise and degrade others—such words belong to the old world that is already passing away in the light of the cross. God's new world, God's new society, is a world in which words uplift, in which words show honor to others—words that give guidance and reverent joy even in hard times. Hateful speech has been the way of the bully from time immemorial, as the story of Nabal shows. There is nothing new about temper tantrums of hate, even on Twitter. Such speech is already now in the past, condemned by God on the cross of Christ; the future of God's new world belongs to words that instruct, words that illumine, words that give the right answer at the right time, words that heal and encourage, brought to light through the resurrection of Christ. Mutual respect lived out in the honor of mutual obligation is God's living will, God's gracious purpose for every human being on the face of the earth, even including the highest levels of human government, perhaps especially there. *There is no excuse*; there *can be* no excuse; hateful speech is *always* wrong, from anybody, anywhere, under any circumstances, at all times. Jesus said—and he was speaking to the religious leaders—"But what comes out of the mouth proceeds from the heart, and this is what defiles. For out of the heart come evil intentions, murder, adultery, fornication, theft, false witness, slander" (Matt 15:18–19). The way of the bully is the way of the fool, then and now, and that applies to everyone.

We consider, second, the politics of Trumpism, in particular his authoritarianism (I alone can fix everything!) and his populist demagoguery (I am the will of the people!). We have described his authoritarianism; Donald Trump is himself the moral compass for all decisions of national life. If it is good for Trump, it is good for the nation; if it is bad for Trump, it is bad for the nation. As the elected leader, he is the national good in one personification, and all laws are to be interpreted as serving his interests. If its serves his interests, it is legal; if it contradicts his interests, it is illegal. Now, some evangelicals, when confronted with Trumpist authoritarianism, tell us that Jesus after all never told Caesar how to run Rome. It is a catchy phrase, belonging on Twitter, or perhaps on the lips of a televangelist. It is also a specious argument, for of course Caesar did not administrate the province of Judea, his legate Herod did. Did Jesus ever speak ill of Herod? Devoted readers of the Bible know that he did, rather forthrightly. When told that Herod was hunting him down to kill him, Jesus called Herod a "fox," and sends word to him that he will go on with his ministry nevertheless in active, peaceful disobedience to his rule (Luke 13:32). "Fox" here is a distinctly unflattering epithet, to say the least; it means a scheming little creature, a conniving pipsqueak, as opposed to a big-hearted lion, a true ruler. Jesus is making it clear that Herod may think he holds all the political power in Judea, but he is mistaken. God holds all power, here and everywhere, and Jesus will continue his ministry, in peaceful but steadfast defiance of Herod's pretensions. Jesus does tell Caesar—or Caesar's representative in Judea—how to run Rome; those who hold political power have it solely on loan from God, who rules and overrules the ways of even the most outwardly aggressive.

But let us once again listen to a larger story concerning the issue of authoritarianism, the story of Naboth's vineyard (1 Kngs 21). Ahab is now king in Israel, and he is sullen and upset. He sulks, morose and complaining. What has put him in such a state? He has everything but he wants more. He has spotted a lovely garden, a vineyard, belonging to a man named Naboth. And he wants it, simply because he doesn't have it. He offers to buy it from Naboth, but Naboth refuses to sell, not out of stubbornness, but because in Israel land cannot be sold outside one's family. Land belongs to God; it is on loan to a family. It is the religious duty of Naboth to keep the vineyard in his family, and he therefore will not sell to the king. Once again a woman enters the story, but this time, unlike Abigail, she makes things worse rather than better. Jezebel the queen sees King Ahab curled up on his bed in a foul mood, refusing to eat, moping and whining, and when she finds out what troubles him, sets out to make things right. She knows the way Ahab governs: he has the absolute right to do whatever he pleases. Why is he not using his power to get what he wants? And so she sets about acquiring the vineyard. Her method is simple. She frames Naboth for a crime he did not commit. It is all carefully orchestrated: letters are written to just the right jurists, false witnesses are procured and paid, and suddenly Naboth is put to death. The law, for Ahab and Jezebel, is simply a tool for power. The law does not govern those who serve, it serves those who govern. Naboth dies; Ahab gets his vineyard; Jezebel is triumphant, as everything goes their way. Until Elijah the prophet comes and asks: "Have you killed and taken possession?" God is over all, and above all; he will not be mocked. Ahab and his house are finished.

Authoritarianism sees equality under the law as a mere inconvenience to be set aside at will. Laws can always be manipulated by those, and for those, who have the most to gain. In the end, the lifeblood of authoritarianism is acquisition of more, always more. The law is a tool to be used by the powerful to acquire yet more and more, and if need be new laws can be passed where old laws stand in the way. God's new world sweeps the world of authoritarianism away, and sets in its place a new society where human dignity flourishes. We are not defined by what we have, nor by the constant, churning need to have still more. Plenty is plenty; enough is enough. We are defined rather by our mutual connections with one another in bonds of respect, honor, and trust. My fellow human being is not an obstacle in my way of acquiring still more and more; my fellow human being is the very definition of my own humanity. We live, together, side by side, with each other, and for each other. My fellow human beings are not simply there to live by my side, they are there as opportunities to show *kindness*. They are neighbors, whether across the street or across the horizon. I will seek to see them not in the worst light but in the best light, and so to show them honor, always giving credit where it is due, always eager to shine light, not throw shade, on the accomplishment of others. Authoritarianism lives by the power of lies: lies that destroy the dignity and reputation of a neighbor in the hidden places of human cruelty. God is truth and light and he forever exposes the lies of humankind, even those from the highest sources, especially those from the highest sources. It is often said that we live in a post-truth world. But that is, from the perspective of the Christian gospel, a misnomer. We live in a pre-truth world. God's new world, God's new society, even now shines the new light of truth that is the true future of all humankind.

Trumpism is a form of populist demagoguery, which we must carefully distinguish from democracy. In democratic society, a leader is elected by majority vote, and then governs *all* the people, those who voted for that leader and those who did not, always careful to protect the rights of the minority, always keeping in mind the good of the society as a whole. Ours is a democratic republic; elected officials serve the common good of all, not those who supported them. For the demagogue—including its Trumpist form, quite clearly—a leader is elected by majority vote, and then works *solely* to the advantage of those who elected them, carefully attacking the interests and representatives of those who did not. Indeed, the demagogue is really not working for the advantage of anyone other than themselves; the more a powerful, fearful, and angry division can be erected between those who are *for* the leader, and those who are *not*, the more likely (so it is believed) the leader can be reelected, in some societies indefinitely. The demagogue has no interest in protecting the rights of the minority, but rather in *eliminating* them. The demagogue has no interest in reaching across the aisle but in doing everything possible to antagonize and stir up political divisions, whether they exist in reality or not, for that feeds the energy of reelection. The demagogue does not exist to govern, and has no competence in doing so; the demagogue exists to *campaign*, endlessly, and that is the only real goal of every government decision. Of course we hear from evangelicals: well, Trump was elected, get over it! He can do what he wants! Why should he worry about what other parties think? He should fight for the people who voted for him! We ask: what does Holy Scripture say about the demagogue?

We are indeed instructed by the story of Absalom, the son of David the king, who leads a popular revolt against the king, and for a time almost succeeds in winning the throne (2 Sam 15–18). As is so often the case in the Bible, we do not learn of Absalom's character in terms of abstract, moral terms. We learn of his character from a small detail: his lavish devotion to his hair. With evident irony—even with a touch of delightful gaudiness—the narrator tells us how Absalom allows his luxurious head of hair to grow for an entire year, every year. Then, at the end of the year, there occurs the great cutting of Absalom's hair, almost a ritual legend. He not only has it cut at the end of every year, he has it *weighed*; there is no one in the whole world that can have more hair than Absalom, and he can prove it! He has the best hair in the world! That is Absalom, self-absorbed to the point of pathology, yet with talent only for expanding his ego outward into the world. His narcissistic character will nearly destroy the kingdom of Israel. He is a master destroyer of worlds.

He knows exactly what to do. First, he needs to be *seen* as a king. Whether or not he is fit to govern is irrelevant; the only thing that matters is the impression, the image. So he hires a professional bodyguard, and rides around Jerusalem with horses clamoring and chariots clattering. It should be noted: this is not the way kings in Israel act; this is the way the pagan kings of the East act, but no matter. Absalom will set a new standard for how a king acts; he will change the face of power in the kingdom. He is the new monarchy! Secondly, he sows seeds of resentment, the true power of the demagogue. He waits by the gate outside the king's palace, and when he spies people coming from the north—outside the traditional home base of David—he calls them over. It is a breach in protocol; they are there to see the king. But no matter—the demagogue has no concern for protocol. This is the new monarchy! He tells the people: there is no one looking out for your interests! He sows chaos, bitterness; he is there to divide, to conquer, to destroy. You will never get justice from this government! They don't care about you at all, but I will! If I am king, I will listen to all your complaints! He "steals their hearts"; they are his, and he is theirs.

And thirdly, he cloaks his actions in piety. He throws a massive feast to fulfill a vow to God. It is all part of the grand conspiracy, as the biblical narrator makes quite clear. Piety is a tool for power, not a service to God. Absalom drives David out of Jerusalem and for a time usurps his throne. But in the end, his sheer incompetence proves his undoing. Fleeing from David's soldiers, his massive head of hair becomes entangled in the branches of a tree, where he dangles helplessly between heaven and earth, a victim of his own insatiable vanity. The vile rebellion is over.

It is of the essence of democracy that it is rule by law, not by persons. Persons may *occupy* an office to which they are voted, but they do not *become* it. Laws are not made by the leader but by an independent legislature. And those laws are not interpreted by the leader, but by an independent judiciary. Authority rests, not on the person, but on the laws, including the offices which those laws outline and circumscribe. The goal of the leader, the executive, is the good of *all* the people. The great enemy of democracy is the attempt of the demagogue to define an in-group and an out-group. In our time that happens most clearly in the form of ethnic-nationalism. The outsiders and intruders must be cordoned off from the centers of power. A wall must be built, at all costs, even to the point of bringing meaningful government to a halt. Such a society is already defeated by the cross of Jesus Christ, which breaks down every barrier dividing one human being from another. In the new society there is a balanced concept of the common good, which does not pit one group against another, but which sees unity strengthened in diversity, and diversity completed only in unity. The new society defeats the demagogue with nothing less than a *new humanity*. The demagogue lives on bitter anger and resentment among people. He has no interest in *interpreting* the anger, in finding the sources of pain, and alleviating the struggles which produce it. Quite the opposite, he wants only to *enflame* the passions of anger still further, for the strength of anger is the only true energy of the demagogue. Whatever the true sources of anger, the demagogue strives to displace that anger onto the "enemies of the people," which are of course nothing more than the political opponents of the demagogue. The state, and the demagogue, are not only inseparable, they are identical.

God's new world is a world of radical kindness. We may indeed hear voices of anger, even resentment. Those voices may be very well speaking from depths of deep hurt and pain we can scarcely imagine. Our goal is not to gain political advantage from those voices, but to practice radical kindness. We withhold judgment, in order to understand, seeking the circumstances of life which are part of every unique human journey. We thrive, not on anger and resentment—though we can listen to it where it comes—but on the joyous music of a just society living in harmony with one another. The demagogue lives off sheer mendacity; there is simply one lie after another, a chain of lies which in the end strangles the body politic and threatens to snuff out its existence. Create crises! Sow chaos! Deny reality! And then lie about it all, including lies about the lies. Yet the overwhelming weakness of the demagogue is shortsightedness. He cannot see further than the next lie; what he lacks, and what the new society thrives on, is *foresight*. The new society lives for the needs of the future, not for the past. Foresight sees obstacles up ahead and charts a way around them. It establishes goals and maps out the steps needed in order to reach them. Foresight coordinates the strengths of the many, in order to establish the good of all. Over against the foresight of true democracy, the demagogue does not stand a chance.

As we have observed in the previous chapter, evangelicalism has wholeheartedly embraced the politics and policies of Donald Trump. We examined several such instances, and now offer a brief response. We begin with the issue of nationalism. According to Trump, America First, and Make America Great Again, are the true epitome of wisdom. And evangelicals agree. They hunt up a verse here, and a verse there, from the Bible, to support their case, and of course pull out a few carefully chosen and misused facts from American history. For example, they argue that the First Amendment does not prohibit the establishment of *any* religion at all; it only prohibits the establishment of any particular Christian *denomination*. America *is* a Christian country, just not Baptist, or

Methodist, or Episcopal. That is common wisdom in evangelical circles; it is also of course historical falsehood of the worst sort, not even worth rebutting. Far more important is the outright neglect of the biblical witness. What does the Bible say about God in his relation to the nations of the earth?

We find all nations included in the promise of God to Abraham: that in him all families and nations will be blessed. Indeed, this great promise is the theme of the entire book of Genesis, as it is passed from one patriarch to another, to Isaac, and to Jacob. It is founded on God's electing love. God alone wills to love his people solely because of his kindness and mercy, not at all because of their great achievements: "It was not because you were more numerous than any other people that the Lord set his heart on you and chose you—for you were the fewest of all peoples. It was because the Lord loved you . . ." (Deut 7:7–8). We learn a lesson about the nature of God's electing love and the nations of the world. God blesses a nation because of his kind mercy, not because of a nation's intrinsic worth; and the *purpose* of that blessing is to be a *means* of blessing for others, never an *end* in itself. The moment Israel sees its own election as an end in itself, the judgment of God rings down from heaven through the voice of the classic prophets of Israel.

Amos thunders: "Alas for those who are at ease in Zion, and for those who feel secure on Mount Samaria, the notables of the first of the nations, to whom the house of Israel resorts! Cross over to Calneh, and see; from there go to Hamath the great; then go down to Gath of the Philistines. Are you better than these kingdoms? Or is your territory greater than their territory, O you that put far away the evil day, and bring near a reign of violence?" (Amos 6:1–3). A nation whose affluent citizens (dwelling in the capitols of Zion and Samaria) live solely in the false security of national self-interest; a nation who divorces itself from moral purpose, and shows callous unconcern for any but themselves; a nation whose proud self-assertion and bragging is shattered by the overpowering might of God Almighty; such a nation is built solely on violence against the poor. Such a nation has only one hope: "Seek good and not evil, that you may live; and so the Lord, the

God of hosts, will be with you, just as you have said. Hate evil and love good, and establish justice in the gate; it may be that the Lord, the God of hosts, will be gracious . . ." (Amos 5:14–15). Only a new passion for social justice can make good the promise of the nation.

Consider the prophet Isaiah, who inveighs against the squeezing out of the poor by the rich: "Ah, you who join house to house, who add field to field, until there is room for no one but you, and you are left to live alone in the midst of the land! The Lord of hosts has sworn in my hearing: Surely many houses shall be desolate, large and beautiful houses, without inhabitant . . ." (Isa 5:8–9). Economic development, if it is carried out on the backs of the poor, is an abuse of power, and will not be established in the land. The wealthy do not see God's hand at work in the world. Their arrogant blindness to God's righteous purpose destroys the nation. The only hope? "Cease to do evil, learn to do good; seek justice, rescue the oppressed, defend the orphan, plead for the widow" (Isa 1:16–17). This is not a general program of national renewal, whether capitalist or socialist, but a series of highly specific imperatives. The nation is complacent, self-righteous, corrupt; it must radically change the concrete direction of life in the most basic, pragmatic sense. Only results matter.

Is the nation saved by the religious leaders, the prophets and the priests? Consider the words of Hosea: "For with you is my contention, O priest. You shall stumble by day; the prophet also shall stumble with you by night . . ." (Hos 4:4–5). The religious leaders are misleading the people, not guiding them. For what is needed is not more religion, but something altogether different: "My people are destroyed for lack of knowledge; because you have rejected knowledge, I reject you from being a priest to me" (Hos 4:6). The answer is not more religion; the answer is the knowledge of God: "They will not hurt or destroy on all my holy mountain; for the earth will be full of the knowledge of the Lord as the waters cover the sea" (Isa 11:9). Notice that the tense here is future. This is not a return to some glorious past. This is a new act of God, a new creation, a new restoration of all things. The *whole earth* now reflects the beauty of God's sovereign blessing.

We condemn the nationalism of Trumpism, and evangelicalism which supports him. It is outright idolatry, and does not fall within the legitimate scope of the gospel. It is false doctrine. Christ the risen and exalted Lord even now holds *all nations* and *all peoples* in his hands. The blessing of God upon our nation, the United States—just as the blessing of God upon *any* and *every* nation—cannot ever be rightly understood as a self-contained good to be hoarded and consumed. Such a society will inevitably lapse into profound injustice. God's blessing upon our country is real; but it is to be seen truly only in the light of God's ultimate purpose for good among all peoples and nations. We are grateful to God for the country in which we live. Yet only if we recognize his hand at work among all peoples and nations will we be truly patriotic citizens of our own, eager to do his will for the good of all.

The evangelical view of Christian Zionism must be rejected by the confessing church of Jesus Christ as false doctrine. The church thoroughly commends and approves the older Zionism of David Ben-Gurion, the steadfast belief in a new country of Israel that is safe for Jewish people, democratic, and oppresses no one. Indeed, according to the apostle Paul, all Israel will be saved (Rom 11:26); all Jews belong to the redeemed community of God. Jews and Christians are joined together as two people in one community of faith; that is the grand biblical vision of divine grace, which lies at the background of Christian concern for modern Israel, and replaces the now discredited notion of supercessionism.[1] But that is not the Christian Zionist belief. We reject the notion of a "Greater Israel" based on the purported borders found in various places (and in various iterations) in the Bible. The tradition of the conquest and settlement of the land recorded in the book of Joshua is without doubt attested in the Bible as the will of God. But it is narrated quite clearly as a *one-time event*, not to be repeated. The theological shape of Scripture never returns to the conquest tradition; the prophets of Israel rather point *forward* increasingly to a new creation by God, encompassing not only Israel but the

---

1. Supercession is the traditional Christian view that the church *replaced* Israel in the divine economy.

entire cosmos. Israel's traditional enemies will not be excluded, but included, in the worship of God in an era of universal peace and reconciliation: "On that day there will be a highway from Egypt to Assyria, and the Assyrian will come into Egypt, and the Egyptian will come into Assyria, and the Egyptians will worship with the Assyrians" (Isa 19:23). True Zionism welcomes everyone, while at the same time securing a homeland for the Jewish people in a democratic state. Such Zionism is to be fully affirmed. But Christian Zionism, when joined to a distorted Israeli policy, will only lead Israel down the road of becoming an occupying force, an apartheid state, permanently occupying the Palestinian people. Christian Zionists care nothing about that eventuality, for they care nothing about the people of Israel. Their only concern is with the details of their apocalyptic timeline, which leads in fact to world war precisely in the Middle East. It is firmly to be hoped that the citizens of Israel, and Jews around the world, will see through the morally vacuous inanity of Christian Zionism, reject it utterly, and in their own hearts and minds return to the original Zionism of peace and justice for all, a vision of such beauty as to thrill every human person of good will. Next year in Jerusalem (*L'Shana Haba'ah B'Yerushalayim*)!

We also reject as false doctrine the entire secular apocalyptic vision of evangelicalism, which since its very roots in the nineteenth century has been a vast misreading of Holy Scripture. The Bible forbids any timeline of events; yet evangelicals have mastered the art of manipulating Scripture to develop baroque and thoroughly unbiblical timelines of politicized propaganda. The Bible subordinates all apocalyptic images to the crucified, risen, and exalted Lord; yet evangelicalism considers the return of Christ just one more item, increasingly seldom mentioned, in an elaborate schema of events that have swallowed up the Christian hope. The return of Christ is not, for the confessing church, just one more item in a schema of events. There is no scheme: there is only the return of Christ, the *one true hope* of the church and the world, for which we wait in eager longing. He will come again! That is our eschatology; all other speculation is to be thoroughly avoided.

The notion that Donald Trump is somehow prophesied in the Bible is an obscenity, an idol, a golden calf. The notion that Donald Trump is Cyrus the Persian prophesied in Isaiah 45 is a crass vulgarity; for it is quite clear in the text of Scripture that Cyrus the Persian is Cyrus the Persian, prophesied by Isaiah, and sent by God to deliver the people Israel by shattering the Babylonian empire. Cyrus the Persian is God's prophesied and appointed deliverer of God's people, a great king; Donald Trump is not.

The entire secular apocalypse of evangelicalism compromises the most basic truths of the Christian faith and witness. It envisions a world in which good and evil are in constant conflict. The Bible, by sharp contrast, makes it fully clear that already Christ the risen Lord rules all things, and all reality is under his sovereign authority. Even evil itself, however tragic and horrible, is made to serve his gracious purpose: "The kingdom of the world has become the kingdom of our Lord and of his Messiah, and he will reign forever and ever" (Rev 11:15). His kingdom is now *concealed*, hidden from the eyes of the world, among the weak, the hungering, the peacemakers, the suffering; but it is fully *real*, and will one day be fully manifest for every eye to see.

There is no room for fear, and the politics of fear; the Christian way is the way of hope, not fear. Hope looks forward, never backward, and it lives now in the light of the new world of God. There is no room for fanaticism, and the politics of fanaticism; the Christian way is the way of faith, which comes by returning and rest, not by restless agitation. There is no room for the politics of division and hate. Christian faith is the way of love (1 Cor 13). We see the world in fragments, says the Apostle Paul. Love is willing to tolerate that ambiguous, fragmented vision in patience and kindness, never rude or boastful or arrogant or envious, never sure that ours is the only right way, never irritable or resentful of others. Christians do not have the right answers to every question; that is the realization of love, and the commitment of love to responsible action in society. While we are here we are daily transformed by love into what we will one day be, in the glory of his kingdom through the return of our Lord. Love alone transforms us, now, into who we will then become. Without love, a so-called Christian politics is nothing more than Christian fascism, which betrays the name Christian, indeed the name of Christ.

While it is not our primary concern, it is crucial to add here a word about the topic of abortion, which is often used by evangelicals as their reason for supporting Trump. Trump himself of course is *deeply* concerned about the issue, at least the last I heard. The issue of abortion did not become the single-issue political bludgeon it is now among evangelicals until the formation of the Moral Majority in 1980. It is one thing to have a firm conviction concerning the morality and legality of abortion, and to stick by it; it is quite another to make that particular issue the *one litmus test* for voting. Indeed, until 1980, there was a wide range of opinion even among evangelicals about the issue. *Roe vs. Wade* passed largely unnoticed by evangelicals. It was only when Francis Schaeffer first sounded the alarm in his *Christian Manifesto* that it become what it is today: an isolated political cudgel, unrelated to the larger complex of moral thinking in which it is imbedded.

What do I mean? First of all, where there is *genuine* concern for abortion, there is genuine concern for unwed mothers. The Scriptures do not turn *any* away; Christ lives a holy life, but he lives it precisely in the midst of the real-life, flesh-and-blood world of human messiness. We hear nothing but "family values"; what about the value of those who have no family, who need help, who are alone and afraid? Where is the evangelical community for them? Why not make support for unwed mothers, and adoption services, the *single issue* around which voting must circle?

Second of all, it is indeed a remarkable fact of human history that the early church stood steadfastly opposed to the horrific Roman practice of infanticide, of exposing unwanted young babies—often girls—to death. The church took in those babies, raised them, and preached against the practice; but they do so as part of a comprehensive *affirmation of life*. They also opposed war and violence of any kind. There are sermons from the early church where it is even asked whether a soldier can be saved. I am not suggesting that soldiers cannot; I am merely pointing out that war was considered so utterly unspeakable to the early church that it was a serious issue whether authentic faith in the gospel was even possible among soldiers. Which evangelical is asking that today? Where are the crowds of evangelicals crying out *against war every-where?* Furthermore, the early church invented—yes invented—the first hospital. In Constantinople, after an outbreak of plague, when the rest of Roman citizens were leaving even their family members for dead in the streets, Christians were the first in line to take the sick in, and constructed a unique institution: a place where doctors and nurses of the time could gather and care for the sick, a hospital. If life in all its forms is precious, then why are evangelicals not the *first in line* to promote every reasonable effort to extend healthcare to everyone? After all, the Bible is filled with miracles of healing; if God's inbreaking rule brings healing in its wings, why don't evangelicals make healthcare for all citizens—for all humanity—the *one highest priority* of their political existence?

And third, if you support the sanctity of life at conception and birth, you must support the sanctity of life at death, and that must apply to everyone. Capital punishment is a crime against the gift of life. Yet why are evangelicals not making the *end of capital punishment* the one litmus test for deciding upon a candidate? The answer to all these questions I fear is a single word: hypocrisy. And it is not hypocrisy simply in the sense of doing one thing, while saying another. That is bad enough. However, in the Bible, hypocrisy goes deeper; it means putting on a mask, playing a role. I do not doubt the genuineness of evangelical concern for the unborn. But wrenched free from the larger culture of life in which such concern is imbedded, it appears all too clear that the issue plays a role: and that is as a *political opportunity.* Let love be genuine, says Paul; and in this case, that means embracing life everywhere it is.

The evangelical rejection of science, and in particular the science of climate change, is to be rejected as false doctrine, together with the notion that humankind is here to dominate earth. Several points need to be made, based on Scripture. First of all, science is not a threat to faith, and never has been. We are made by God to inquire, to understand, to investigate: "whatever is true, whatever is honorable, whatever is just, whatever is pure, whatever is pleasing, whatever is commendable, if there is any excellence and if there is anything worthy or praise, think about these things" (Phil 4: 8). These are words of *culture*, including science; *think about these things*. Don't ignore them; don't build walls of ignorance and alternative "Christian" science against them. Rather, give them some serious thought: that is the mainstream Christian attitude to modern science (and modern culture generally). In particular, there is unambiguous consensus among scientists that the earth is warming at a catastrophic rate, and that the primary cause is human use of fossil fuels. These are facts, not debating points for uninformed religious pundits.

Now, the Christian faith does have something unique to contribute to the human conversation about climate change, though it is radically different from evangelical denial. We hear a great deal about human responsibility for the environment, and that is certainly better than irresponsibility; but infinitely better is the wisdom of Scripture. "The earth is the Lord's and all that is in it, the world, and those who live in it; for he has founded it on the seas, and established it on the rivers" (Ps 24: 1). The world of creation, the world of nature, *does not belong to humankind;* it belongs to God. That is the Christian witness. We should approach it, therefore, not so much with eager responsibility to make things right, as with overpowering humility and awe in the face of God's grandeur. It is not ours; it is *his*. Yet he has given us sun, and wind, and water; and from these we can easily tap the solar power, the wind energy, and the hydro-electric power, to make human life fully human, and reverse the course of human destruction of our planet. The abundant gifts of creation are there: we are fools if we do not receive and use them. We have learned the techniques of nonviolence against the forces of radical evil in society; it is time to use those same techniques to thwart radical evil against the destruction of God's own world.

Trumpism is a politics of division, of hate, of fear. By definition, it requires a hostile other, which it creates simply by defining it into existence. As we have seen, there are two forms of the other.

The first is an overt, external other, and that is the immigrant. Trumpism sees immigrants—by which it means immigrants from the South and from Islamic countries—as enemies. America is truly America only when it is protected from such outsiders, who are invading our country. It is all a lie of course; there is no "invasion." There are now and always have been issues of immigration policy to handle and discuss; but the essence of Trumpism is precisely *not* to handle and discuss them, but to inflame and breed chaos where order is required. And evangelicalism has—to its profound discredit—followed Trumpism straightaway. It has turned, within a very short time, from its own historic openness to immigrants, to a closed-minded and closed-hearted anti-immigrant fear and hatred. The logic needs to be observed. First the politics of the party into which evangelicalism has been completely absorbed—the GOP—changed its approach to immigration, during the first decade of the new millennium, then evangelicalism dutifully followed right behind. Finally, as if on cue, it "found" its new orientation in the Bible. The evangelical interpretation of "illegal" vs. "legal" immigration in the Bible is a perfect example of the logic of confirmation. The distinction is made by the political party; then in coordination (*Gleichshaltung*) the religious wing of the party looks for ways to make it sacred. There is no such distinction in the Bible of course. No translators, no readers, no commentators, no theologians, have ever seen it, until the Tea Party formed in 2010; and then suddenly there it is! Just like the German Christians who had to produce a new version of the New Testament without Judaism to accord with the requirements of the political climate of the time, so evangelicals now have their anti-immigrant Bible. The logic is frankly shameful.

What does the Bible say about immigrants? As we have mentioned, it actually says quite a lot. Indeed, in many passages it is made quite clear that our faith, indeed, our very standing before God almighty, is measured by how we treat immigrants. There is a distinction in the Bible between two types of immigrant, but it is not "legal" versus "illegal," a modern invention thoroughly unknown to the world of Scripture. Rather, the distinction is between the stranger, that is one who is passing through a country or city and may or may not stay for awhile (sometimes translated as sojourner), and the resident alien, that is one who comes from elsewhere to a new land or city and settles and becomes part of the new people or society. The important point is that the social status, and the religious or theological status of the two, is *identical* in the Bible. What is said about the former is said about the latter; what is said about the latter is said about the former. The distinction is a minor one, and as soon as it is made is all but abandoned. A stranger is a stranger; an immigrant is an immigrant; that is the witness of the Bible.

So, what does the Bible say about these strangers, these sojourners, these resident aliens, these passing guests? There are three layers of theological reflection in the Bible. All are crucial, though not all are always carefully observed. We cannot simply count the references, though they are many: the various words for immigrant/stranger occur well over 100 times in the Old Testament, and quite often in the New Testament. Moreover, the issue of the immigrant is deeply imbedded in several narratives of the Bible, and is the subject matter of an entire book, that of Ruth. In fact, when Jesus preaches his very first sermon to his hometown synagogue in Nazareth, and announces the astounding truth that he is himself the mystery of God's coming rule, right here, right now, present in their midst, they reject him. So he reminds them of the Old Testament truth that God's overreaching grace often comes foremost to foreigners, to strangers, to the outsiders: "But the truth is, there were many widows in Israel in the time of Elijah, when the heaven was shut up three years and six months, and there was a severe famine over all the land; yet Elijah was sent to none of them except to a widow at Zarephath in Sidon. There were also many lepers in Israel in the time of the prophet Elisha, and none of them was cleansed except Naaman the Syrian" (Luke 4:25–27). The pious people of his hometown are used to hearing traditional moral values, and are not pleased. In fact they are so enraged they try to kill him. This is not a minor issue in the Bible; we cannot merely count the references, but need to weigh them theologically.

The first truth for our reflection is our status before God, and that is, that we are, in his sight, *all immigrants*. This is not mystical poetry; this is a confession of our utter dependence upon God for all things, and our basic sense that God, and God alone, is ultimately our home. Consider these words from the psalter: "Hear my prayer, O Lord, and give ear to my cry; do not hold your peace at my tears. For I am your passing guest, an alien, like all my forebears" (Ps 39:12). None of us—not a single one of us—is *entitled* to ask God for *anything*. We live by his grace. We live by his mercy. We live upon the earth that he has made, and that belongs to him alone, not to us. We are not entitled to demand blessings, or protection, or deliverance. We are immigrants, guests, sojourners in his world. We rely solely upon his freely given grace and mercy, his loving kindness, his favor. We come to him not as the strong, but as the weak, who know that he alone is our strength. He answers our prayers because of his love, overflowing, abundant, marvelous to behold. Similarly, this verse: "I live as an alien in the land; do not hide your commandments from me" (Ps 119:19). As immigrants, as aliens, on God's good earth, we depend utterly and completely upon him to know his good will in all things. Abstract moral norms; so-called moral absolutes; worldviews; such are all worthless, and less than worthless, in his sight. The one thing that matters is this: to *know God's will*, and to do it. *His commandment* alone is good, and we do not deserve to know it. He commands as he wills, and then gives as he commands. Finally, consider this: "Lord, you have been our dwelling place in all generations. Before the mountains were brought forth, or ever you had formed the earth and the world, from everlasting to everlasting, you are God" (Ps 90:1–2). God alone is our home. This is not a mere metaphor; the deepest treasures of life we find in him, and in him alone; that is why we are permanent exiles, permanent resident aliens, permanent immigrants on earth. We can only issue a blunt warning: those who find their deepest truth in homeland, blood and soil, *lose God*. By contrast, those who live in God their home, in whom we live and move and have our being, sit loose on the things of this world, even including—perhaps in the light of the ethnic-nationalism of our time especially including—the idols of the tribe.

From the first truth follows the second truth. God's people in the Bible are, quite literally, an immigrant people, not just in the theological sense, but in the very real social and political sense. It begins, as most things do, with father Abraham: "Now the Lord said to Abram, God from your country and your kindred and your father's house to the land that I will show you" (Gen 12:1). It is not the case that Abraham becomes an immigrant, and then finds the blessing and promise of God. Quite the opposite. The *promise of God* breaks the life of Abraham away from everything familiar to him: his native land, his wider loyalty to his extended family, and even to his own intimate family. That same promise brings Abraham to a new land, where he is a nomad, a wanderer, a sojourner, and remains so all his life. His one possession in the land is a field and a cave where he can bury Sarah his beloved wife and companion under the promise; but even in buying it he is cheated by the native inhabitants, paying an exorbitant price, a small piece of biblical witness to the common lot of the immigrant at the mercy of native inhabitants (Gen 23). They know it; he knows it; he knows that they know it; but he buys it anyway, a small down payment on God's ultimate promise. Isaac and Jacob remain immigrant exiles in the land of promise; and finally the entire people of God are forced into slavery in Egypt, where they are immigrants, "resident aliens" according to Stephen's recitation of the sacred story just before his death (Acts 7:6). Yet the crucial point is: when they come to the promised land, when they inherit the blessing and live and dwell in the new land of Canaan, they *forever remain immigrants*. The Scriptures are quite clear on this point: "for the land is mine; with me you are but aliens and tenants" (Lev 25:23). They do not come into the land of promise as immigrants, and then suddenly *own* the land as natives, as citizens. Yes, the land is given to them by God's promise, but the promise always remains gracious, a gift. Even on their *own land* they are resident aliens, immigrants once and always. The New Testament of course continues the same theme, especially in the book of Hebrews. Summarizing the entire trajectory of the people of God in the Old Testament, the text concludes: "All of these died in faith without receiving the promises, but from a distance they saw and greeted them. They confessed that they were strangers and foreigners on the earth, for people who speak this way make it clear that they are seeking a homeland. If they had been thinking of the land that they had left behind, they would have had opportunity to return. But as it is, they desire a better country, that is, a heavenly one. Therefore God is not ashamed to be called their God; indeed he has prepared a city for them" (Heb 11:13-16). The second point thus circles back to the first. Precisely because we are never fully at home in a world of blood and soil, we recognize our homeland in God alone; or better, precisely because we recognize our home in God, we will never, ever, be at home in a world defending blood and soil against the outsider. *We are the outsider.* Yes, we are grateful, active, and responsible citizens of our country, glad patriots of a noble nation. But, we sit loose, always looking "forward to the city that has foundations, whose architect and builder is God" (Heb 11:10).

The second truth leads to a third truth. How we stand before God is manifested by our treatment of immigrants. Once again the Scriptures are quite clear. Above all, the unambiguous testimony of the Old Testament, repeated in endless and various iterations, is that immigrants—strangers, sojourners, resident aliens—are to be treated the same as everyone else. And the reason is always the same: because you know what it is like to be an immigrant. You have been there. They are not to be wronged or oppressed: "You shall not wrong or oppress a resident alien, for you were aliens in the land of Egypt" (Exod 22:21). It is not simply that God's people have known the status of immigrant; they carry in their *very feelings* the scars and wounds: "You shall not oppress a resident alien; you know the heart of an alien, for you were aliens in the land of Egypt" (Exod 23:9). There is here not simply the absence of maltreatment; there is the requirement of mutual support and mutual sharing of life's goods: "Then you, together with the Levites and the aliens who reside among you, shall celebrate with all the bounty that the Lord your God has given to you and to your house" (Deut

26:11). Again and again, it is reiterated in dozens of different ways and contexts, that there is to be only one law that applies equally and the same to all, including immigrants: "As for the assembly, there shall be for you and the resident alien a single statute, a perpetual statute throughout your generations; you and the alien shall be alike before the Lord. You and the alien who resides with you shall have the same law and the same ordinance" (Lev 15:15–16). The New Testament of course draws these threads together, and reads them in the light of the incarnation. Jesus Christ himself *is* the immigrant, the stranger, the sojourner, the resident alien in our midst; how nations treat them is how they treat him. And how they treat him, is how they are to be judged in the final judgment before God, whether as sheep at his right hand, or as goats at his left (Matt 25:31–46). I was a stranger, an immigrant; that is the word of Christ to the nations. Did you welcome me? That is the question of Christ to all peoples of the earth.

What kind of immigration policies follow from these reflections? I am a theologian, not a legislator. I can only assume that any policy would include a modern system of border security; a humane and deliberative processing procedure; a full and robust integration of new immigrants into American society. But above all, any true policy would necessarily reflect the fact that *we are an immigrant nation.* We are not citizens on the inside, and immigrants on the outside; we are, in the very depths of our history, immigrants. We always have been, and we always will be, and we forget it to our own destruction as a vibrant culture and society, a shining light upon the earth. It is not for nothing that our national symbol is the Statue of Liberty, which is there *to welcome immigrants*, with the immortal lines of Emma Lazarus: "A mighty woman with a torch, whose flame is the imprisoned lightening, and her name Mother of Exiles." True freedom is the welcome of exiles; that is the mystery of Christ among us.

We conclude our study with a brief reflection on the issue of race. It is no secret to anyone that racism has been endemic to American history and society. Until 1865, that racism took the form of slavery, the legal ownership of one human being by another. Slaves from Africa were used by white Americans to build and develop the nation. *Used* is the right word; they were treated, not as human beings, but as possessions, to be deployed at will. The institution was an execrable disgrace to humanity, and was finally ended, but only after a Civil War; but the civil war did not end racism, it only ended slavery. The hideous ugliness of racial prejudice simply morphed into new forms: into Jim Crow laws, into segregation, into the Ku Klux Klan, into lynching, into laws against miscegenation, into systematic suppression of the voting rights of blacks. It is remarkable to consider that it was only in the mid-1960s that the United States became a multicultural country. The civil rights era—and new legislation opening the door to immigration from the South and other parts of the world in 1965—first made the idea of a genuinely multi-racial, multi-ethnic, multicultural society possible. It is of course against this very idea that Trumpism is directed with its well-known slogan.

Until 1965, America was, de facto, a white supremacist society. Trumpism is the effort to bring back and retain that white supremacy in the present. The catalyst was simple: a black man was elected president of the United States, and for whites like Trump that was the unspeakable horror. Sadly, white evangelicalism has followed him in this crusade. Both Trump and evangelicalism personally abused Obama with hideous lies and insults, garnered from the dark spaces of conspiracy theories and the alt-right. Trump now speaks of the countries from which African Americans came as shitholes; Franklin Graham lectures African Americans about obeying police as if they are newly freed slaves in need of social instruction. Trumpism, and white evangelicalism, are united as one in this: they are threatened by the new multiculturalism that is America, and they want to continue their hegemony, their dominance, their rightful place. Trump wants white supremacy; evangelicals want white Christian supremacy. Each will support the other to the bitter end to insure what they want, no matter what the cost. Supremacy is the goal; race is the problem; and any means necessary are to be used.

Who is my neighbor? The question of course is asked of Jesus, and he responds with the parable of the Good Samaritan (Luke 10:25–27). As familiar as it is, it is often misconstrued; a fresh hearing is helpful.

A lawyer comes to speak with Jesus. He is a religious leader, schooled in the Scriptures, especially the moral code. He is not coming with an open mind; he is coming to prove Jesus wrong. He asks the most basic moral question: what must I do to inherit eternal life? Jesus, as he often does, turns the question back on to the listener: you are a scholar of the Bible, you tell me. Love for God, and love for neighbor, this lawyer responds; that is what the law requires. Jesus agrees, but he adds a crucial point: *do* this, and you will live. *Knowing* is one thing; doing is quite another. There is still a question hanging in the air, and the lawyer asks it: okay, who is my neighbor? We see where he is headed. He wants to prove that he is right; he wants to make it clear that he *has* fulfilled the will of God. His point is clear: you have to draw the line somewhere. I know all about love, but you can't go around loving everyone. So tell me, Jesus, where exactly do you draw the line when it comes to love? In answer, Jesus tells the parable of the Good Samaritan. It will end, not with an answer, but with a question. As is often the case, Jesus questions the questioner.

A certain man is walking along the road from Jerusalem to Jericho. The stretch of road, some twenty miles, passes through rocky desert, deserted and lonely. Notoriously, robbers and violence were a common threat to travelers. And so it happens: this man is robbed, beaten, and left for dead on the side of the road. By coincidence, two religious figures pass by, one by one, perhaps after doing their religious duties in Jerusalem. These two, the priest and the Levite, have privileged status in society because of their religious positions. They do not even bother to check on the man to see if he is alive. With heartless disregard, they keep walking, even careful to move to the other side of the road. "This is not my concern!"

A third man comes, a Samaritan. Now we need to know one crucial fact about this, and all, Samaritans: they were regarded by

Jewish people at the time with outright hatred. He sees the injured and broken man, and is instantly moved by deep concern. He takes action, of a decisive sort. He uses his provisions as medicine to soften the wounds, and perhaps begin the healing process. He lifts the man upon his mount, and takes him to a nearby public inn. He has taken care of his present needs, but his concern does not stop there. He insists that the innkeeper watch over the man in his care, and promises to pay whatever costs are incurred. The contrast between these actions by the despised Samaritan with the treatment given by the religious leaders could hardly be greater.

Then comes the question of Jesus, which makes the whole point of the story clear. The lawyer has asked: who is my neighbor? He wants limits, boundaries, a clear and definite direction as to just how far love can and may go, thus far and no further. For the lawyer, a neighbor is the *object* of one's love. The neighbor is someone I care for; and the only question is, which limits must I obey in the range of such objects?

It is crucial to recognize that Jesus *changes* the question entirely. He does not ask: was the injured man on the road truly a neighbor? That would be to play the game of the lawyer, to fall into the trap of approved lists of people to love. He asks a very different question: who *acts* as neighbor to the man who fell among robbers? For Jesus, *being a neighbor* is radically different, radically new, in the light of God's encroaching realm. A neighbor is not an *object* of my concern. The one who *helps* is the neighbor. The person who shows concern, the person who *acts* like a neighbor to others, is the neighbor. The lawyer had asked: who *is* my neighbor? looking for an approved list of people. Jesus asks: who *acts* like a neighbor, defining a new way of being in the world. And the lawyer can only answer: this despised Samaritan, he is the one who acts like a neighbor. He—not the religious leaders—he is the one who showed kindness, who showed mercy. Indeed, the lawyer cannot even bring himself to say the word: the Samaritan. Jesus concludes: you, you go out and act like this Samaritan. You go and *be a neighbor* to others.

Piety then, and piety now, makes lists of approved people to help. Sure, we will help these people over here, but we would be fools to help those people over there! Those are not *our* people! These people are my neighbors; but those people, well, are just *different*. These people have our same ethnic heritage, our same national origin. I can love these people; but those people? Piety makes assumptions about *those* people, and much of the time, perhaps most of the time, perhaps all of the time, those assumptions are simply false. Those who look like us; those who think like us; those who share our "cultural heritage"—these are our true neighbors, surely! We will love them and help them, so help us God! This is love of neighbor as an *object*; love that is quantified; and in the light of God's new world, is no love at all.

The radical love of Christian discipleship means a lot of things, but above all here it means love without approved lists, love *without restrictions* in the world. Love goes beyond all boundaries, as the parable of the Good Samaritan amply illustrates. It goes beyond any racial-ethnic boundaries, being neighborly wherever the need arises. It goes beyond any religious boundaries, for all are creatures of the same God, made in his image. It goes beyond national boundaries, for all the nations of the world are precious in his sight. It goes beyond cultural boundaries, for being a neighbor sees the genuine humanity in everyone. Who acts as neighbor in the world? The one who sees a need, and without regard to any lists of approved piety, simply shows the needed kindness and mercy, with absolute and total disregard for the social consequences of approval or disapproval by social norms. The one who willingly and even gladly crosses every boundary for the sake of humanity is the true neighbor, for Christ the King already now holds in his love every human being on the earth, for whom he died and rose again.

The church of Jesus Christ is at home in a multicultural, multi-racial, multi-ethnic society. It *thrives* there. The Apostle Paul draws out the implications of grace for God's new world: "There is no longer Jew or Greek, there is no longer slave or free, there is no longer male and female; for all of you are one in Christ Jesus" (Gal 3: 28). We have *no desire* to turn the clock back. We despise the efforts of those who would use the gospel for their cultural agendas of regression and oppression. We do not look backward; we look forward, always forward, until that day when all time is swallowed up in the victory of the cross.

Bibliography

Althaus, Paul. *Die Christliche Wahrheit*. Gütersloh: Bertelsmann, 1952.
Barth, Karl. *Theological Existence Today*. Eugene, OR: Wipf and Stock, 2011.
———. *The Word of God and the Word of Man*. New York: Harper and Row, 1957.
Bergen, Doris L. *Twisted Cross*. Chapel Hill, NC: University of North Carolina Press, 1996.
Bonhoeffer, Dietrich. *Dietrich Bonhoeffer Works* 12. Translated by Isabel Best and David Higgins. Minneapolis: Fortress, 2009.
Bowler, Kate. *Blessed*. Oxford: Oxford University Press, 2013.
Brody, David, and Scott Lamb. *The Faith of Donald Trump*. New York: HarperCollins, 2018.
Busch, Eberhard. *The Barmen Theses Then and Now*. Grand Rapids: Eerdmans, 2010.
———. *Karl Barth*. Translated by John Bowden. Philadelphia: Fortress, 1976.
Clark, Victoria. *Allies for Armageddon*. New Haven, CT: Yale University Press, 2007.
Ericksen, Robert P. *Theologians Under Hitler*. New Haven, CT: Yale University Press, 1985.
Fea, John. *Believe Me*. Grand Rapids: Eerdmans, 2018.
Fitzgerald, Frances. *The Evangelicals*. New York: Simon and Schuster, 2017.
Grudem, Wayne. *Christian Ethics*. Wheaton, IL: Crossway, 2018.
———. *Politics According to the Bible*. Grand Rapids: Zondervan, 2008.
Hagee, John. *Earth's Last Empire*. Franklin, TN: Worthy, 2018.
Heschel, Susannah. *The Aryan Jesus*. Princeton, NJ: Princeton University Press, 2008.
Hirsch, Emanuel. *Gesammelte Werke* 32. Waltrop: Hartmut Spenner, 2006.

Bibliography

Jones, Robert P. *The End of White Christian America*. New York: Simon and Schuster, 2016.

King, Martin Luther, Jr. *Strength to Love*. Minneapolis: Fortress, 2010.

Noll, Mark. *God and Race in American Politics*. Princeton, NJ: Princeton University Press, 2008.

Pelikan, Jaroslav, and Valerie Hotchkiss, eds. *Creeds and Confessions of Faith in the Christian Tradition*. 3 vols. New Haven, CT: Yale University Press, 2003.

Solberg, Mary. *A Church Undone*. Minneapolis: Fortress, 2015.

Strang, Stephen E. *God and Donald Trump*. Lake Mary, FL: Charisma House, 2017.

Sutton, Matthew Avery. *American Apocalypse*. Cambridge, MA: Harvard University Press, 2014.

Ustorf, Werner. *Sailing on the Next Tide*. Berlin: Peter Lang, 2000.

Whitman, James Q. *Hitler's American Model*. Princeton, NJ: Princeton University Press, 2017.